Gendered Perspectives on Community College

Jaime Lester
EDITOR

Number 142 • Summer 2008
Jossey-Bass
San Francisco

GENDERED PERSPECTIVES ON COMMUNITY COLLEGE
Jaime Lester (ed.)
New Directions for Community Colleges, no. 142

Arthur M. Cohen, Editor-in-Chief
Richard L. Wagoner, Associate Editor

NEW DIRECTIONS FOR COMMUNITY COLLEGES (ISSN 0194-3081, electronic ISSN 1536-0733) is part of The Jossey-Bass Higher and Adult Education Series and is published quarterly by Wiley Subscription Services, Inc., A Wiley Company, at Jossey-Bass, 989 Market Street, San Francisco, California 94103-1741. Periodicals Postage Paid at San Francisco, California, and at additional mailing offices. POSTMASTER: Send address changes to New Directions for Community Colleges, Jossey-Bass, 989 Market Street, San Francisco, California 94103-1741.

SUBSCRIPTIONS cost $85.00 for individuals and $209.00 for institutions, agencies, and libraries in the United States. Prices subject to change. See order form at the back of book.

EDITORIAL CORRESPONDENCE should be sent to the Editor-in-Chief, Arthur M. Cohen, at the Graduate School of Education and Information Studies, University of California, Box 951521, Los Angeles, California 90095-1521. All manuscripts receive anonymous reviews by external referees.

New Directions for Community Colleges is indexed in CIJE: Current Index to Journals in Education (ERIC), Contents Pages in Education (T&F), Current Abstracts (EBSCO), Ed/Net (Simpson Communications), Education Index/Abstracts (H. W. Wilson), Educational Research Abstracts Online (T&F), ERIC Database (Education Resources Information Center), and Resources in Education (ERIC).

Microfilm copies of issues and articles are available in 16mm and 35mm, as well as microfiche in 105mm, through University Microfilms Inc., 300 North Zeeb Road, Ann Arbor, Michigan 48106-1346.

CONTENTS

Editor's Notes

In 1995, Barbara Townsend edited a volume of *New Directions for Community Colleges* on gender and power in the community college. She and the chapter authors described the situation of women in community colleges and examined the influence of large numbers of women on two-year institutions. Beginning with the premise that gender representation, power, and stereotypes are significant in organizations, each chapter highlighted how a discussion of women leaders, students, and faculty affects and is affected by gendered perspectives. Townsend's volume has served as one of the only complete resources for individuals interested in examining the relationship among social identities, power, and the community college. A decade old, it now seems appropriate to reexamine gender in the community college setting and continue a discussion of the importance of female representation and experiences in our nation's two-year colleges. In addition, a discussion of gender should also include the perspective and lived experiences of males. Therefore, this volume both extends the work in Townsend's volume and broadens the discussion of gender to masculinity.

Issues of gender within a community college setting are always relevant. We know that the numbers of women in community college have not dramatically changed over the years. Large numbers of women have continued to enter the community colleges as faculty, administrators, staff, and students. Moreover, community colleges continue to be the place in the postsecondary hierarchy with the largest proportion of female workers. Women have been almost equally represented in faculty ranks in two-year institutions and have experienced unique opportunities to advance in administrative positions (DiCroce, 1995; Jablonski, 1996; McKenney and Cejda, 2000; Mott, 1997; Nidiffer, 2003; Phillippe, 2000; Piland and Giles, 1998). For example, women occupy up to 38 percent of the community college president positions, and 29 percent of women lead California's community colleges (McKenney and Cejda, 2000; Phillippe, 2000; Piland and Giles, 1998). In 2003, women were found to make up approximately 38.3 percent of faculty in higher education but 49.2 percent of faculty in community colleges (National Center for Education Statistics, 2003).

The issue of what gains women in community colleges have made is complex. Although these women are doing better relative to women in four-year universities with respect to presidential appointments, men continue to dominate the presidential role (Harvey and Anderson, 2005). Women of color have also made significant gains in the administrative ranks at community colleges relative to four-year institutions, but they are well below

NEW DIRECTIONS FOR COMMUNITY COLLEGES, no. 142, Summer 2008 © 2008 Wiley Periodicals, Inc.
Published online in Wiley InterScience (www.interscience.wiley.com) • DOI: 10.1002/cc.319

parity, with only 5.7 percent minority women presidents at the community college level. The inclusion of women in some aspects of community colleges appears to illustrate that community colleges are gender equitable; yet the actual number of women in leadership positions and the exclusion of women of color point to a lack of equity. This complex picture of gender in community colleges creates a need to continue to examine the unique gender-equity issues in two-year institutions.

The importance of gender extends beyond statistical measures of representation. Research on these women's paths to leadership positions, gender identity conflicts among faculty, and recent discussions of men and masculinity speak to multifaceted gender-related experiences within higher education (Amey, 2006; Harper, 2004; Lester, forthcoming). Of note are the current national debates on the shrinking numbers of men in undergraduate education and attention to men of color. Gender socialization, masculinity, and the experiences of men within higher education institutions provide evidence of the ways in which men struggle to matriculate in college. In addition, a discussion of masculinity contributes to the debate on community colleges as gender-equitable institutions and extends the singular focus from femininity to the inclusion of masculinity. Without a discussion of men and masculinity, we are unable to fully understand why gender equity has not been achieved. Finally, the exclusion of men ignores a large population within the community colleges that is also susceptible to gender roles and norms. Therefore, this volume seeks to continue and expand the research on women in community colleges while also addressing issues of gender more broadly to include the experiences of men.

This volume explores the gender issues of community colleges and begins to unravel the complexities of gender for both men and women in two-year institutions. The chapters examine a wide range of gender-related issues that speak to the current challenges of community colleges. Many two-year colleges struggle with faculty retention and impending retirements of large numbers of faculty and leaders. In order to hire and retain new faculty, a discussion of work-life balance and the experiences of women leaders synthesizes ways in which community colleges can change policies and practices to develop leaders and retain faculty. Also included is a discussion of faculty work-life balance and representation of women in campus and districtwide governance. A challenge that all community colleges face is the need to serve students from various backgrounds. This volume provides a discussion of the gender-related experiences of female and male students, providing evidence of and recommendations for new ways to serve students who may be struggling with identity issues. Community colleges face a variety of challenges that are uniquely related to gender. This volume synthesizes many of the new challenges and provides extensive recommendations of how community colleges can assist those who teach, learn, and lead in our nation's democratic colleges.

This *New Directions for Community Colleges* volume is useful to several audiences. It provides faculty and leaders with an alternative perspective of their work environments that illuminates issues related to gender. Leaders who are interested in creating more pluralistic cultures that are welcoming to men and women will be interested in the issues of work-life balance, the satisfaction of noninstructional staff, and the gender identity conflicts that male students face. Faculty should consider the discussion of governance and the need to advocate for greater inclusion of faculty from across the institution, such as part-time faculty. In addition, this volume will be of interest to graduate students and scholars who are concerned with issues of gender, seek alternative perspectives of community colleges, and are interested in the intersection of workplace cultures and social identities. A discussion of gender in community colleges appeals to a wide range of individuals who seek to create and recommend practices and policies that make our nation's democratic colleges welcoming, diverse, and successful.

Chapter One, by Barbara K. Townsend, provides an overview of the gender equity issues that community colleges face today. In a discussion of the changes to gender equity issues since her *New Directions* volume in the mid-1990s, Townsend describes the new trend of considering issues of gender as they affect both men and women. Gender equity is no longer a simplistic view of examining issues related to women, but a look at the impact of multiple and intersecting identities on students, faculty, and staff. Community colleges that are ethnically diverse and have students from a variety of socioeconomic backgrounds are uniquely challenged to look beyond simple notions of gender. Townsend elaborates on the new focus on work-family balance among faculty and staff. The new generation of faculty and staff at community colleges is generally more concerned with work-life balance, necessitating that two-year colleges look to support faculty and staff beyond the workplace. Finally, Townsend summarizes the gains in gender equity that have occurred in community college since the mid-1990s. Using measures of representation, salaries, and faculty demographics, she shows that community colleges have made great strides in becoming more equitable for women.

The next two chapters focus on issues related to men and masculinity and community colleges. In Chapter Two, Athena I. Perrakis provides evidence of the factors associated with academic success for African American and white men. To do so, she uses a large, urban community college district as a backdrop with the purpose of illuminating the unique experiences of men in higher education. Chapter Three, by Frank Harris III and Shaun R. Harper, takes a different approach from that of Perrakis. These authors use gender socialization and the literature on masculinity to engage in a discussion of the gender identities that men bring to college. They also look at the identity conflicts that affect male students' attitudes, behaviors, and retention. The vignettes of the four students in the chapter illustrate the interaction of gender identity, masculinity, and college experiences that potentially contributes to the lower numbers of men in undergraduate education. Chapters Two and Three contribute to the debates on the representation of men in higher education by identifying the challenging issues that men face as college students.

Chapter Four, by Soko S. Starobin and Frankie Santos Laanan, which also focuses on students, addresses the scarcity of women in science, technology, engineering, and mathematics (STEM) fields in community colleges. Similar to their four-year counterparts, community colleges have low numbers of women who enter STEM fields, which leads to a small number of women students who transfer to STEM programs in universities. Understanding what causes STEM retention in community college provides further evidence of the leaks in the proverbial STEM pipeline. Data from a project funded by the National Science Foundation provide qualitative evidence of the importance of learning experiences, interactions with faculty, and educational and career aspirations on the overall impact of women in STEM fields. Starobin and Laanan conclude with compelling suggestions for practice, including the need to build a supportive community for women STEM students, send positive messages about women in STEM, and advise students correctly so that they can see a clear pathway to the baccalaureate.

Chapters Five and Six turn to issues related to noninstructional staff and faculty in community colleges. Despite their importance as financial aid and admissions officers and their high level of contact with students, noninstructional staff have been almost completely ignored in the research literature. The vast majority of these staff are women, indicating that this group is ripe for an analysis of gender issues. In Chapter Five, Molly H. Duggan focuses on organizational climate and workplace satisfaction among noninstructional staff to illuminate the impact of gender on interactions with faculty and students and perceptions of the workplace. Chapter Six, by Jaime Lester and Scott Lukas, continues to explore satisfaction but does so among faculty in campus and districtwide governance. The literature on gender, faculty, and governance points to the exclusion of women in high-power governance committees, as well as a lack of power in the decision-making process. Using California's 109 community colleges as a site for the study, Lester and Lukas provide evidence of gender-based discrimination during involvement and participation in governance.

The next two chapters present evidence on the challenges that leaders and faculty face in community colleges. In Chapter Seven, Pamela L. Eddy and Elizabeth M. Cox use interviews with six current women presidents of community colleges to unravel their experiences. The rich data portray women who are seeking to exist by adapting their leadership style to suit the masculine culture. This chapter illustrates community colleges as gendered organizations and a male-normed organizational structure. Margaret W. Sallee in Chapter Eight extends the discussion of gender equity to faculty and work-family balance. Research notes that women faculty enter community college because they want to establish work-family balance (Townsend, 1995). As Townsend describes in Chapter One of this volume, a new generation of faculty is valuing work-family balance. The data provided by Sallee's survey illustrate that community college faculty feel supported by their institution, but also have fewer resources to draw on to establish work-family balance. Sallee offers important suggestions for practice of ways that community colleges can easily be more family-friendly.

Chapter Nine takes a different approach to discussions of gender in community colleges by examining compliance with Title IX. Cindy Castañeda, Stephen G. Katsinas, and David E. Hardy use national data to systematically understand if community colleges are measuring up to Title IX standards. They extend the discussion of gender equity beyond notions of faculty and administrative representation and salaries. The final chapter, by Pamela L. Eddy and Jaime Lester, concludes the volume with a discussion of the lessons learned from Chapters One through Nine. The authors summarize several of the pressing issues faced by community colleges, such as the attack on affirmative action and the expansion of gender construction. These issues show a need to establish new policies and practices within community colleges to better serve students and provide a welcoming and pluralistic workplace for faculty and staff.

Community colleges today face a variety of challenges that extend beyond representation and other numerical measures of equity. This volume provides practical recommendations and potential solutions to continue to foster equity in our nation's democratic colleges.

Jaime Lester
Editor

References

Amey, M. J. *Breaking Tradition: New Community College Leadership Programs Meet 21st Century Needs.* Washington, D.C.: American Association of Community Colleges, 2006.

DiCroce, D. M. "Women and the Community College Presidency: Challenges and Possibilities." In B. K. Townsend (ed.), *Gender and Power in the Community College.* New Directions for Community Colleges, no. 89. San Francisco: Jossey-Bass, 1995.

Harper, S. R. "The Measure of a Man: Conceptualizations of Masculinity Among High-Achieving African American Male College Students." *Berkeley Journal of Sociology,* 2004, *48*(1), 89–107.

Harvey, W. B., and Anderson, E. L. *Minorities in Higher Education, 2003–2004: Twenty-First Annual Status Report.* Washington, D.C.: American Council on Education, 2005.

Jablonski, M. "The Leadership Challenge for Women College Presidents." *Initiatives,* 1996, *57*(4), 1–10.

Lester, J. "Performing Gender in the Workplace: Gender Socialization, Power, and Identity Among Women Faculty." *Community College Review,* forthcoming.

McKenney, C. B., and Cejda, B. D. "Profiling Chief Academic Officers in Public Community Colleges." *Community College Journal of Research and Practice,* 2000, *24,* 745–758.

Mott, M. C. "Women Community College Presidents' Leadership Agendas." Unpublished doctoral dissertation, University of Arizona, 1997.

National Center for Education Statistics. *Background Characteristics, Work Activities, and Compensation of Instructional Faculty and Staff.* Washington, D.C.: U.S. Department of Education, 2003.

Nidiffer, J. "From Whence They Came: The Contexts, Challenges, and Courage of Early Women Administrators in Higher Education." In B. Ropers-Huilman (ed.), *Gendered Futures in Higher Education.* New York: State University of New York Press, 2003.

Phillippe, K. A. *National Profile of Community Colleges: Trends and Statistics.* Washington, D.C.: Community College Press, 2000.

Piland, W. E., and Giles, R. "The Changing Face of the California Presidency." *Community College Review,* 1998, 25(4), 35–43.

Townsend, B. K. (ed.). *Gender and Power in the Community College.* New Directions for Community Colleges, no. 89. San Francisco: Jossey Bass, 1995.

JAIME LESTER is assistant professor of higher education at George Mason University.

1

This chapter compares the concept of a gender-equitable community college in the 1990s and today.

Community Colleges as Gender-Equitable Institutions

Barbara K. Townsend

In the mid-1990s, I edited a *New Directions for Community Colleges* volume on gender and power in the community college (Townsend, 1995b). One of the chapters explored the extent to which women community college faculty members were on the margins in academe and within the community college itself (Townsend, 1995c). Over a decade later, I have been asked to assess the extent to which community colleges today are gender equitable. In this chapter, I do so by reflecting on how gender relations and gender equity were viewed in the 1995 volume. I then describe how I see early twenty-first-century perceptions of gender relations and gender equity.

Gender and Power in the Mid-1990s

Gender and Power in the Community College reflected the assumptions of liberal feminists who came of age during the second wave of feminism. We assumed that gender is socially constructed in such a way that women are disadvantaged socially, politically, and economically (Townsend, 1995a). We also assumed that "the power affecting gender relations within an institution is primarily structurally based" (p. 2), meaning that institutional gender relations are shaped by those holding positional power within the institutional hierarchy. As part of this assumption, we contended that this power is sometimes deliberately and sometimes inadvertently used to maintain stereotypical gender relations.

WILEY InterScience® DISCOVER SOMETHING GREAT

NEW DIRECTIONS FOR COMMUNITY COLLEGES, no. 142, Summer 2008 © 2008 Wiley Periodicals, Inc.
Published online in Wiley InterScience (www.interscience.wiley.com) • DOI: 10.1002/cc.320

Our assumptions about gender and power were typical ones used in analyses of gender relations at four-year institutions, although we focused on the community college. We also were typical in thinking about gender equity in terms of the percentage of women students, faculty, and administrators, especially presidents, and looking for parity in numbers.

In the mid-1990s, women were well represented in the community college as students, as faculty, and, to a lesser extent, as presidents. As in the four-year sector, women students were in the majority, as they have been since the late 1970s. However, female faculty members were more prominent in community colleges than in the four-year sector: 45 percent of full-time two-year college faculty were women as compared to 34 percent in the four-year sector (Perna, 2003). Women presidents were also more prevalent in the community college than in four-year institutions (American Council on Education, 1995).

Although the community college was full of women in various roles, these women still appeared to experience some gender inequities. In the aggregate, female faculty members were paid less than male faculty members and were also less likely to be tenured (Perna, 2003). However, when Perna examined 1993 National Study of Postsecondary Faculty (NSOPF) data and controlled for various structural variables such as field of study and unionization status, differences in salary, tenure status, and rank disappeared. Thus, Perna concluded that among full-time community college faculty with similar levels of education and experience, there were no gender differences in salary.

Similarly, gender inequity in presidential leadership was apparent because the percentage of women presidents was not at parity with that of male presidents. At the same time, the presence of female presidents was increasing substantially from previous decades: in 1975, there were 45 women presidents as compared to 102 in 1984 (Epstein and Wood, 1984). By 1995 women filled approximately 20 percent of the presidencies of accredited two-year colleges. In addition, the increase among women community college presidents was occurring at a faster rate than in four-year institutions.

Thus, we concluded that gender relations at community colleges were likely to be more positive than in the four-year sector. Women students were in the majority, and they found many women faculty in the classroom. These faculty members, coupled with female presidents and administrators, provided role models for women students.

Nevertheless, we still perceived that gender relations needed improvement. Some of the recommendations we made to alter the power dynamics affecting gender relations included having student affairs "adopt a feminist perspective that would view women's needs as central rather than peripheral to the community college" (Townsend, 1995a, p. 3), "empowering women by changing or modifying curricular programs and services and organizational structures" (p. 3), and "connecting the characteristics of [women community college presidents'] gender to the power of their office" (p. 4). I concluded that "the community college needs to be responsive to the actual, not stereotypically conceived, needs of female *and male* [italics added] students, faculty, and administrators" (p. 4). However, this inclusion or mention of men was not typical in the volume.

As I look at these recommendations from the perspective of 2008, I believe that the final recommendation of responding to everyone's need, regardless of gender or position within the community college, foreshadowed what is happening currently.

Gender Equity in the Twenty-First Century

This current volume, *Gendered Perspectives on Community Colleges*, shares some of the focus of the 1995 volume but also reflects a somewhat different perspective about gender relations. In common with the first volume, this one examines several areas in which gender inequities persist to the disadvantage of women. It addresses continued inequities in the representation of women leaders and in the small number of women students in certain disciplines. However, some of the inequities are in areas not discussed in the first volume: inequities in women faculty's participation in decision making, the treatment of professional staff, and gender inequities in community college athletics. In addition, this new volume clearly focuses on both genders, with two of its ten chapters looking specifically at community college male students. Finally, this volume includes an emerging issue of finding balance between work and family, a topic only indirectly addressed in the 1995 volume and one that applies to both female and male faculty.

Focus on Both Genders. This volume's focus on both genders is consistent with an overall shift in higher education to consider gender issues as affecting both men and women. In the mid-1990s, many scholars who looked at gender issues were still concentrating on the needs of women. By the turn of the century, higher education scholars had begun to look at the effect that high female enrollment and participation in certain curricula had on male students. For example, Serex and Townsend (1999) surveyed how one university's male students in the gender-atypical majors of nursing and education perceived the classroom climate.

As the twenty-first century began, the gender gap became defined as a declining percentage of male students relative to female students, whether traditional age or nontraditional age. As evidence, the percentage of male traditional-age undergraduates declined from 47 percent in 1995–1996 to 45 percent in 2003–2004. Among older or nontraditional-age students, men are outnumbered by women almost two to one (King, 2007). As a result, some four-year colleges and universities have decided to accept male students at a higher rate than female students so as to achieve relative gender parity. For example, the College of William and Mary in 2006 accepted 26 percent of its female applicants as compared to 44 percent of its male applicants to achieve a student group that was 54 percent female. It is important to note that the community college, as an open admission institution, does not participate in efforts to alter the percentage of male students admitted to its student body.

The decline in the percentage of male undergraduates has been interpreted by some as meaning that "women's success hinders men's success" (Williams, 2007, p. 1), that "equality for girls means inequality for boys" (Musil, 2007, p. 1), and that "success for girls and women deprives boys and men of the chance of success" (p. 1). In other words, gender equality is construed by some to be "a zero sum game" (King, 2007, p. 7).

This simplistic view of gender relations, however, ignores student gender gap differences by race, ethnicity, and income. "Significant gender gaps favoring women did not develop within each racial and ethnic group until the mid-to late-1990s" (King, 2007, p. 5). Among low-income traditional-age students, the enrollment gap between male and female students is most apparent: white and Hispanic female enrollment is higher than for similar male students. There is no gender gap in undergraduate enrollments of white, upper-income traditional-age male and female students (King, 2007, p. 3). In addition, while enrollments of women students are increasing, their socioeconomic status as a group has declined in the past few decades. A recent national study by Sax and Arms (2008) found that four-year college male and female students had similar socioeconomic backgrounds in the 1960s. "Since 1966, however, median family incomes for male students have increased by approximately 40 percent, relative to a 17 percent increase among the women" (p. 28). Thus, more women students may be attending college, but in the aggregate, they experience greater financial concerns than do male students in the aggregate.

Although enrollment of women students in the aggregate has increased in the past few decades, there has been little change in the percentage of women students who enroll in fields with high wages. These fields are typically considered nontraditional ones for women and include areas such as engineering technologies, precision production, and mechanics of transportation. Women students continue to dominate enrollments in traditionally female fields such as nursing and allied health areas like dental and medical technician (Bailey and others, 2003).

Work-Family Balance. Another difference in twenty-first-century discussions of gender relations is the focus on balance of life for both female and male faculty members. In the mid-1990s, this issue was hinted at in the community college when women faculty spoke of choosing to work at the community college because doing so enabled them "to combine having a career with raising families" (Townsend, 1995c, p. 42). They shared that they did not want to deal with the publish-or-perish pressure at research universities and some four-year colleges. The lack of research and publication requirements at the community college enabled them "comfortably to achieve professional fulfillment, sometimes combined with raising a family" (Townsend, 1998, p. 660).

By the twenty-first century, there was a stream of literature calling for greater balance in life for faculty and staff (Center for the Education of Women, 2005). Some of this concern may reflect academe's escalating tenure demands. Even at lower-tier four-year colleges, faculty members are now expected to publish regularly and seek grants. As a consequence, some believe that "a tenure-track career is inconsistent with a meaningful and full family life" (Drago, 2007, p. C3).

Current concern with having a balanced life also reflects a generational change in what matters for women (Kezar and Lester, 2007). Many women who participated in the second wave of feminism (the 1960s through the early 1980s) believed that gender equality would occur when women achieved numerical parity with men, whether as students, faculty, or administrators. This generation of feminists focused on organizational change, including the development of women leaders who would change organizations through their feminist values (DiCroce, 1995). To obtain leadership positions in organizations, women during this time period accepted the need to sacrifice family time. Indeed, some women "were willing to forgo having children or marriage for career advancement" (Kezar and Lester, 2007, p. 12).

In contrast, women reflecting third-wave feminism (from the mid-1980s to the present) are less willing to take time away from their families to achieve institutional change through leadership positions. They are "searching for a balance between work and personal life that they believe was lacking in their parents' lives" (Kezar and Lester, 2008, p. 12). As a result, they want institutions to facilitate child rearing by creating a room where women can pump breast milk and providing child care on campus. In other words, women influenced by third-wave feminism are open and vociferous about their needs as women faculty (Wolf-Wendel, Ward, and Twombly, 2007). Their approach is very different from that of earlier generations of feminists, especially liberal feminists who sought to be treated like men. Second-wave feminists wanted equal pay for equal work and equal opportunities for advancement but did not emphasize their differences from men. Women reflecting the third wave of feminism also want these conditions for women, but the context in which they seek these conditions has changed. Their context includes three successive decades in which women have dominated undergraduate enrollments and the percentage of women faculty and senior-level administrators has increased significantly.

Changing Higher Education Context for Women. At the community college, women account for the majority of students and have parity in the faculty ranks, even at the full professor level. In 2003, full-time women faculty accounted for 49 percent of full-time community college faculty (Cataldi, Fahimi, and Bradburn, 2005) and in 2005–2006, 50.8 percent (West and Curtis, 2006). No other higher education institution has this high a percentage of full-time female faculty members. In addition, female faculty members in two-year colleges are almost as likely to be tenured as are male faculty: over 62 percent of women as compared to over 68 percent of men. Also, a far higher percentage of community college women faculty members is tenured than are women faculty in four-year public or private colleges and universities: 62 percent versus 38.5 percent. The percentage of full professors who are female is almost 47 percent in the community college as compared to 19 percent in doctoral institutions, 28 percent in master's-level institutions, and 29 percent in baccalaureate institutions (West and Curtis, 2006).

Women senior-level administrators are more prevalent in the community college than in four-year institutions. Almost 28 percent of two-year college presidencies were held by women in 2004. In comparison, less than 18 percent of four-year college presidents were female in 2005 (Chronicle of Higher Education, 2005). In addition to a growing percentage of women college presidents, there are high percentages of women leaders in other senior positions at the community college. As of 2002, 42 percent of chief academic officers were female, as were 55 percent of student affairs officers, 30 percent of chief financial officers, 45 percent of chief continuing education administrators, 29 percent of directors of occupational and vocational education, and 49 percent of business and industry liaisons (Amey and VanDerLinden, 2002).

Another aspect of the current context in which third-wave feminism exists is the virtual elimination of gender differences in community college faculty salaries. On the average, women full-time community college faculty earn between 4 and 7 percent less than do their male counterparts, and in some institutions they earn more. The 2006 national salary study of the American Association of University Professors found that among the 183 associate degree–granting colleges that had faculty ranks, twenty-four (13 percent) had a higher average salary for women faculty than for men (West and Curtis, 2006). In contrast, women faculty members at four-year institutions earn between 11 and 22 percent less than male faculty members (Curtis, 2004).

A major reason for the greater equality of male and female faculty salaries at the community college may be the criteria used for salary decisions. In contrast to four-year institutions, over half the community colleges use the highest degree held as "the primary basis for determining compensation for full-time teaching faculty" (College and University Personnel Association, 2007, p. 7). And over 20 percent use academic rank as the main criterion, which works well for female faculty since the percentage of female faculty holding the rank of full professor is almost equal to that of male faculty.

Conclusion

In sum, the context in which today's community college women—whether administrators, faculty, or students—function is one where women are everywhere. Women students have many female faculty and administrative role models, women full-time faculty members are at virtual parity with their male colleagues in terms of numbers and tenure status and salary, and women administrators are highly likely to be supervised by and to supervise women administrators.

As a consequence, twenty-first-century community college women can move beyond the twentieth-century issues of parity in numbers and salary and focus on what will improve their lives as women, not just as gender-neutral individuals. Calls for comprehensive family leave policies, institutional child care, stopping of tenure clocks for pregnancy or family care needs, and acknowledgment of women as mothers by providing rooms for pumping breast milk reflect women's assertion that women students, faculty, and staff have special needs in the workplace. Equitable treatment of women no longer means treating them like men but rather acknowledging and accommodating their special needs.

Whether by accident or design (Townsend and Twombly, 2007), the community college has led higher education in developing parity on two fronts of major concern to liberal feminists: equal opportunity for career advancement and equality of pay. Whether the community college will also lead the way in meeting the needs of twenty-first-century women in the community college remains to be seen. Since some of these needs intersect with the needs of men, for example, providing child care on campus and improving family leave policies for faculty and staff, the community college now has the opportunity to demonstrate what was recommended in *Gender and Power in the Community College*: being "responsive to the actual . . . needs of female and male students, faculty, and administrators" (Townsend, 1995a, p. 4).

References

American Council on Education. *Women Presidents in U.S. Colleges and Universities.* Washington, D.C.: Office of Women in Higher Education, 1995.

Amey, M. J., and VanDerLinden, K. E. *Career Paths for Community College Leaders.* Washington, D.C.: American Association of Community Colleges, 2002.

Bailey, T., and others. *The Characteristics of Occupational Sub-Baccalaureate Students Entering the New Millennium.* Washington, D.C.: U.S. Department of Education, 2003.

Cataldi, E., Fahimi, M., and Bradburn, E. M. *2004 National Study of Postsecondary Faculty Report on Faculty and Instructional Staff.* Washington, D.C.: U.S. Department of Education, 2005.

Center for the Education of Women. *Family-Friendly Policies in Higher Education: Where Do We Stand?* Ann Arbor, Mich.: Center for the Education of Women, 2005.

Chronicle of Higher Education. "A Chronicle Survey: What Presidents Think, 2006." *Chronicle of Higher Education,* Nov. 5, 2005, pp. 37–39.

College and University Personnel Association. *Community College Faculty Survey for the 2006–07 Academic Year.* Knoxville, Tenn.: College and University Professional Association for Human Resources, 2007.

Curtis, J. *AAUP Faculty Salary and Distribution Fact Sheet 2003–04.* Washington, D.C.: American Association of University Professors, 2004.

DiCroce, D. "Women and the Community College Presidency." In B. K. Townsend (ed.), *Gender and Power in the Community College.* New Directions for Community Colleges, no. 89. San Francisco: Jossey-Bass, 1995.

Drago, R. "Harvard and the Academic Glass Ceiling." *Chronicle of Higher Education,* Mar. 30, 2007, p. C3.

Epstein, C., and Wood, C. L. "Women in Community College Administration." *Community and Junior College Journal,* 1984, *55*(2), 19–22.

Kezar, A., and Lester, J. "Leadership in a World of Divided Feminism." *Journal About Women in Higher Education,* 2008, *1*(1), n.p.

King, J. E. "Featured Topics: Gender Equity in Higher Education: 2006." *On Campus with Women,* 2007, *35*(3), n.p. Accessed Feb. 1, 2008, at http://www.aacu.org/ocww/volume35_3/feature.cfm?section=2.

Musil, C. M. "Director's Outlook." *On Campus with Women,* 2007, *35*(3), n.p. Accessed Feb. 1, 2008, at http://www.aacu.org/ocww/volume35_3/feature.cfm?section=2.

Perna, L. "The Status of Women and Minorities Among Community College Faculty." *Research in Higher Education,* 2003, *44*(2), 205–240.

Sax, L., and Arms, E. "Gender Differences over the Span of College: Challenges to Achieving Equity." *Journal About Women in Higher Education,* 2008, *1*(1), 23–48.

Serex, C., and Townsend, B. K. "Student Perceptions of Chilling Practices in Sex-Atypical Majors." *Review of Higher Education,* 1999, *40*(5), 527–538.

Townsend, B. K. "Editor's Notes." In B. K. Townsend (ed.), *Gender and Power in the Community College.* New Directions for Community Colleges, no. 89. San Francisco: Jossey-Bass, 1995a.

Townsend, B. K. (ed.). *Gender and Power in the Community College.* New Directions for Community Colleges, no. 89. San Francisco: Jossey-Bass, 1995b.

Townsend, B. K. "Women Community College Faculty: On the Margins or in the Mainstream? In B. K. Townsend (ed.), *Gender and Power in the Community College.* New Directions for Community Colleges, no. 89. San Francisco: Jossey-Bass, 1995c.

Townsend, B. K. "Women Faculty: Satisfaction with Employment in the Community College." *Community College Journal of Research and Practice,* 1998, *22*(7), 655–662.

Townsend, B. K., and Twombly, S. "Accidental Equity: The Status of Women in the Community College." *Equity and Excellence in Education,* 2007, *40*(3), 208–217.

West, M. S., and Curtis, J. W. *AAUP Faculty Gender Equity Indicators 2006.* Washington, D.C.: American Association of University Professors, 2006.

Williams, J. "The Visible Man: Moving Beyond Gender Wars to Build Diversity." *On Campus with Women,* 2007, *35*(3), n.p. Accessed Feb. 1, 2008, at http://www.aacu.org/ocww/volume35_3/feature.cfm?section=2.

Wolf-Wendel, L., Ward, K., and Twombly, S. "Faculty Life at Community Colleges: Perspectives of Women with Children." *Community College Review,* 2007, *34,* 255–281.

BARBARA K. TOWNSEND is professor of higher education and director of the Center for Community College Research at the University of Missouri-Columbia.

2

This chapter examines factors that predict and promote academic success, defined as grade point average and course completion, among African American and white male students in a large, urban community college district.

Factors Promoting Academic Success Among African American and White Male Community College Students

Athena I. Perrakis

Community college student demographics have changed dramatically over the past five decades. The system has grown tremendously during this time; large cities have experienced population surges that have transformed and in some cases overwhelmed community college campuses. Interestingly, recent demographic studies, national education statistics, and admissions data reveal that fewer male students of any race or ethnicity are enrolling in college, a trend that is roughly three decades old. Dwindling enrollment of male student populations across the country has raised questions about male student persistence (Evelyn, 2002). Those men who do enroll in college are not completing as many degrees (baccalaureate or associate) today as they did ten to fifteen years ago (National Center for Education Statistics, 2005). The problem of reduced male representation in college is complicated by race; while men in every racial category are earning fewer college degrees now than ever before, some groups are faring better than others. The following questions arise: Who is underperforming, and why? Are there factors related to success for some populations that might also be associated with success for others? And how can community colleges, in particular, work to facilitate degree completion among male students in the light of reduced enrollment?

This study seeks to isolate factors associated with academic success, operationalized here as grade point average (GPA) and course completion,

NEW DIRECTIONS FOR COMMUNITY COLLEGES, no. 142, Summer 2008 © 2008 Wiley Periodicals, Inc.
Published online in Wiley InterScience (www.interscience.wiley.com) • DOI: 10.1002/cc.321

among two male student populations within the Los Angeles Community College District (LACCD): African American and white men. In order to determine the factors that are associated with academic success, two levels of analysis were conducted. The first set of analyses determined if gender was a significant factor in course completion and GPA for all students in the LACCD. Then the study sample was split by gender, and secondary analyses were conducted to determine if race was a significant factor for men in the LACCD, and if so, what similarities and differences could be noted between African American and white male students with regard to course completion and GPA. The result is a set of factors that promote course completion and high GPAs for both African American and white male students.

Review of the Literature

Thomas Mortensen, a senior scholar at the Center for the Study of Opportunity in Higher Education, notes that the statistics for men and women attending college have almost reversed since the 1970s, when 56 percent of students who earned bachelor's degrees were men and 44 percent were women (Brownstein, 2000). Mortensen argues that feminists have silenced the debate regarding the apparent disadvantage men now face in college, noting that the idea of women as disadvantaged in higher education was once true but no longer is. Gose (1999) concurs that people aware of the gender shift on college campuses have not, before now, felt comfortable speaking about it for fear of feminist backlash. However, the achievement gap between men and women is becoming harder to ignore. In the LACCD, total male enrollment across racial and ethnic categories has dropped significantly over the past three decades. In 1974, seventy-six thousand male students were enrolled across the nine district campuses, compared to only forty-eight thousand in 2007. These figures are echoed in many other districts across the country and hint at a pattern of generalized male attrition.

In 1998, 133 women received a bachelor's degree for every 100 men in the United States (Evelyn, 2002). More recent data point to increasing gender disparity in terms of degree completion (National Center for Education Statistics, 2005). Statistics like these are attracting widespread attention of officials at four-year colleges and universities; however, the gap between genders at the community college level has only recently begun to generate much scholarly concern (Evelyn, 2002). Research shows that community colleges remain the predominant entry point for postsecondary instruction among students of color, in particular, among African American students. Traditional theories of retention and involvement have been useful in providing a basis for current research but need to be developed further to uncover the interaction of factors—race, class, gender—that influence retention for diverse students in diverse institutions. Scholars like Bill Tierney call for a new theory of persistence and retention, more sensitive to difference and more capable of reflecting subtle processes involved in the development and retention of students who reflect the new majorities and minorities in American higher education (Rendon, Jalomo, and Nora, 2000).

Levin and Levin (1991) reviewed the student characteristics claimed to have the largest impact on at-risk students in their article on academic retention programs: academic preparedness, adaptability, commitment to educational goals, perception of progress toward educational goals, willingness to seek academic assistance, self-confidence, and reasons for pursuing a college degree. In particular, they note a high correlation between parental socioeconomic status and level of education with retention (Levin and Levin, 1991). Barajas and Pierce (2001) also note that successful students are often those who are seen as having assimilated to the dominant norms and values of the majority culture, in society or on campus.

African American Male Retention

Of all students in higher education, African Americans have the lowest male-to-female ratio (Cuyjet, 2006). African American college students in general, and African American men in particular, face specific challenges after enrolling at predominantly white campuses. One documented challenge is a demonstration of problems associated with strain theory, which posits that a strain develops in an individual who realizes that the products and pleasures of life available to other members of society are personally out of reach (Ellis, 2002). Rather than buy into an ideology of external dominance or superiority, some African American men adopt a nihilistic perspective that all values and beliefs can be dismissed as enigmatic and worthless (Ellis, 2002). Meaninglessness and powerlessness are the initial conditions out of which student alienation and attrition develop (Cabrera and Nora, 1994).

Once African American men begin to define their identities in opposition to the dominant culture of a particular college or university, a stronger likelihood emerges that they will feel alienated and subsequently engage in oppositional behaviors; this process dramatically reduces the likelihood of degree completion (Ellis, 2002). Since black men in American society already confront major challenges to success at all levels of education and are subject to lowered expectations by educational professionals, researchers are working to determine what factors facilitate success for this population and how institutions might remedy the problem of widespread African American male student attrition (Hagedorn, Maxwell, and Hampton, 2001). Such factors might counteract oppositional and counterproductive behaviors that African American male students tend to exhibit in predominantly white educational settings, thereby enhancing their chances for social and economic mobility, especially if implemented in the community college setting where job skills and requisite training for employment are offered (Pope, 2006).

The number of black students enrolled in two-year colleges and the overall poor transfer rates among black students to senior institutions reinforce how serious the problem of attrition has become for African Americans.

According to 2005 National Center for Education Statistics data, black men have earned 5 percent fewer baccalaureate degrees since 1990. The same data set reveals that black men have earned 5 percent fewer associate degrees in the past seventeen years. Yet 3 percent more African American men today remain enrolled in community colleges after five years from the date of first matriculation. Given that the average time to transfer for an entering full-time community college student is three years, a student who remains on a community college campus after five years is statistically less likely to transfer. Pope (2006) affirms the lack of transfer evidenced by black students, noting that in 2002, African American students earned only 10.7 percent of all associate degrees awarded, even though they represented 12 percent of the total community college student enrollment.

Hagedorn, Maxwell, and Hampton (2001) observe that African American men who feel capable of college-level work tend to complete the second semester of their freshman year in greater proportions than those who feel less capable; they are also more likely to persist to degree completion. Social support, defined as "perceived instrumental or expressive profusions supplied to the individual by confiding partners, social networks, and the greater community," is also correlated to persistence and completion for African American male students (Lin, Dean, and Ensel, 1986, cited in Jay and D'Augelli, 1991). Outreach efforts to promote student disclosure of problems once they arise may help students who have difficulty recognizing that a problem exists, asking for help when they become aware of a problem, or asking for help in time for assistance to be of real benefit (Levin and Levin, 1991). Again, these efforts are particularly important for black men who are unlikely to reach out to counselors or college staff when they feel isolated or alienated on campus (Pope, 2006).

Methods

This study employed a quantitative approach to research by using data collected from five thousand surveys distributed by the Transfer and Retention of Urban Community College Students (TRUCCS) project team at the University of Southern California. A quasi-experimental design was used to test the relationship between campus representation of white and black male students as minority populations and academic success. This is a secondary analysis of data that have been gathered, analyzed, and validated through the TRUCCS project. The final sample for this study consisted of 4,333 students from all nine colleges within the LACCD who participated in the TRUCCS survey and for whom transcript data could be acquired. For purposes of this analysis, these students became the experimentally accessible population from which data about white and black students were obtained. The number of white male students within this sample is 6.1 percent of the total sample; black men comprise 4.2 percent of the total sample.

Factor analyses were conducted to determine which variables would be included in multiple regression equations. Twenty-one variables emerged and were regressed on the two dependent variables, course completion and college GPA, which for the purposes of this study are employed as proxies for student success. The first set of analyses was conducted on the entire sample, with a block of interactions to determine, first, what variation in course completion and GPA was explained by the independent variables and, second, whether gender was a significant factor in course completion or GPA. Following this set of analyses, the sample was split by gender. The second set of analyses was conducted only on male students in the sample, again to determine, first, what variation in course completion and GPA for men was explained by the independent variables and, second, to determine whether race was a significant factor in course completion and GPA. Once race was determined to be significant, independent sample *t*-tests were conducted to isolate specific mean differences between black and white men in relation to variables found to be significant for male students through multiple regression analysis.

Findings

Regression analyses conducted on the entire sample of students from the LACCD revealed that some variables were significant for men and women, while others were significant only for one gender (Table 2.1).

At the outset, the researcher expected variables related to socioeconomic status, employment status, and race to be significant for men but not for women. This turned out not to be true. Uniquely significant to men in the sample was a feeling of belonging on campus, which was not significant for female students. Race, age, high school GPA, calculus completion, reasons for enrollment, and dedication to persistence were significant for both genders in the sample.

For the variables of significance to men, a *t*-test was conducted to determine mean differences between the African American and white men in the sample. White and black men are similar in age (twenty to twenty-four years and twenty-three to twenty-six, years respectively), and both are similarly unsure whether they belong on campus. This is not surprising given how low their representation is on the nine LACCD campuses, where in some cases there is less than 5 percent representation of black or white men. Both groups had an average B– high school GPA, and both agree that is important to achieve their goals and complete their degrees. The main difference between African American and white men on these nine campuses is in academic preparation and performance. On average, twice as many white men have completed calculus as black men. White male students were also found to have a college GPA of .398 points higher than black students, a difference of roughly one-half grade. The difference in math achievement may explain in part the difference in college GPA.

Table 2.1. Variable Significance by Gender

Variables Not Significant for Either Gender	*Variables Significant for Women but Not for Men*	*Variables Significant for Men but Not for Women*	*Variables Significant for Both Men and Women*
Occupational status	Marital status	Feeling of belonging on campus	Caucasian
Being the primary wage earner	Intent to succeed academically		Age
Number of children			High school GPA
Others' opinions of the college			Calculus completion
Peer and faculty opinions of the college			Reasons for enrollment
Likelihood of transfer			Dedication to persistence
Highest degree desired			
Perceived obstacles to graduation			
Leisure activities			
Employment status			
Friends enrolled on the same campus			
Difficulties associated with race			

Discussion

This study found that a series of factors alone and in combination predict the academic success of male students (regardless of race) in the LACCD. At the outset of this project, an assumption was made that gender and race would be primary factors in the success and achievement of male students in the LACCD. It was surprising to learn that academic preparation was more significant than race or gender for students in this sample. The majority of the literature in higher education focuses on differences that have historically divided students; the findings of this study highlight the unexpected homogeneity of the LACCD student population. Two-year college students in southern California are more alike than they are different. Although there are obvious gender and racial differences among students attending the nine campuses, these differences do not directly influence student outcomes.

This analysis reinforces how much students are alike in their fundamental desire to succeed in college despite the stereotypes about difference that researchers assume serve as obstacles to their success. Black and white male students feel similarly inclined to complete their courses and degrees; they are roughly the same age; both conclude that others' perceptions of the college they attend are not particularly meaningful or important; and both feel somewhat welcomed on the campuses where they are enrolled. Although the TRUCCS sample is diverse, similarities between African American and white men underscore the importance of promoting retention for all male students regardless of race or ethnicity.

Recommendations for Practice

Based on the findings of this study, the following are recommendations for practice:

- Consider the needs of male students in developing campus activities or workshops. For example, male students are less likely to solicit assistance or engage with counselors on campus, so direct outreach efforts targeted at male students would be beneficial.
- Develop mechanisms to make male students feel more welcomed on campus, and provide them with more of a sense of belonging. Ways to do this might include the creation of a fraternity-type organization where male students can interact with a common interest that is not solely academic but that bonds them with the campus nonetheless.
- Develop a series of day and evening programs targeted to male students so that students attending at different times of day can participate regardless of their off-campus schedules.
- Encourage mentorship by offering incentives for male faculty and male students to eat together on campus or work on common research projects. Male students need to see same-sex faculty and administrators as role models, and extracurricular relationships can help students bridge the gap between students' academic and personal lives.

Conclusion

Hagedorn, Perrakis, and Maxwell (2006, forthcoming) published a pair of papers and corollary lists of positive and negative commandments for the community colleges to indicate ways in which community colleges help or hinder student success. Within the positive commandment list, the authors included faculty-student interaction as one of the ways colleges meet student needs. Within the negative commandment list, the authors noted that students need places on campus where they can study, congregate, and develop relationships. Both of these items address the variable within this analysis that was significant for all men across the nine campuses: a sense of belonging on campus. Male students need to feel a sense of attachment to the campus where they attend classes.

Never before has there been such a significant drop in the number of male students enrolled in institutions of higher education, so the need to maintain services and environments conducive to male success and achievement has not been as pronounced. Given the outcome of the analyses conducted here, policies and practices can be created to advance the interests of all men regardless of race to improve the enrollment and retention of male students. In short, this study suggests that if a policy or practice increases the enrollment and retention of white men, it is similarly likely to increase the enrollment and retention of black men and vice versa.

Beyond race and gender, policy is needed to examine and explore the role of academic diversity in college enrollment and retention. More funding and administrative expertise is needed to understand the academic spectrum of students who attend classes within the LACCD and other similar urban community college districts. As Hagedorn (2003) explains, much remains misunderstood about concurrent enrollment, reverse transfer, and postbaccalaureate enrollment. Differences in levels of academic preparation may in fact supersede differences in race and gender; research and policy is needed to better understand and assist students at different levels of their academic careers. For now, emphasis remains on traditional measures of difference—race, class, gender—while these other categories of difference remain largely unexplored in the literature or institutional policy.

Fundamentally, the most distinct form of diversity within this particular community college district is academic diversity, or diversity in preparation for college-level academic course work. If, as Hagedorn (2003) argues, academic diversity supersedes the importance of race, class, and gender as categories of significant difference among college students, a new model of student retention may emerge that foregrounds academic over demographic factors in predicting student outcomes and facilitating student achievement. Therefore, programs aimed at promoting adequate academic training for college courses will be beneficial in the process of retaining male students. The results of this study are also generalizable to other large, urban community college districts in metropolitan cities, where demographic changes are having a significant impact on student populations. Regardless of how many students of a particular race or gender are enrolled, however, this study reinforces that students who are well prepared for college will outperform their peers with less preparation regardless of their race or ethnicity.

References

Barajas, H. L., and Pierce, J. L. "The Significance of Race and Gender in School Success Among Latinas and Latinos in College." *Gender and Society*, 2001, *15*(6), 859–878.

Brownstein, A. "Are Male Students in Short Supply, or Is This 'Crisis' Exaggerated?" *Chronicle of Higher Education*, Nov. 3, 2000, p. A47.

Cabrera, A. F., and Nora, A. "College Students' Perceptions of Prejudice and Discrimination and Their Feelings of Alienation." *Review of Education, Pedagogy, and Cultural Studies*, 1994, *16*, 387–409.

Cuyjet, M. C. *Preface.* In M. C. Cuyjet and Associates (eds.), *African American Men in College.* San Francisco: Jossey-Bass, 2006.

Ellis, C. M. "Examining the Pitfalls Facing African American Males." In L. Jones (ed.), *Making It on Broken Promises: African American Male Scholars Confront the Culture of Higher Education.* Sterling, Va.: Stylus, 2002.

Evelyn, J. "Community Colleges Start to Ask, Where Are the Men? 151 Women Receive Associates Degrees for Every 100 Men Who Do." *Chronicle of Higher Education,* Jun. 28, 2002, p. A32.

Gose, B. "Colleges Look for Ways to Reverse a Decline in Enrollment of Men." *Chronicle of Higher Education,* Nov. 26, 1999, p. A73.

Hagedorn, L. S. "Seeking the Definition of Academic Diversity in the Community Colleges: Highlights from the Transfer and Retention of Urban Community College Students Project (TRUCCS)." *Urban Ed,* Spring 2003, pp. 14–15.

Hagedorn, L. S., Maxwell, W., and Hampton, P. "Correlates of Retention for African American Males in Community Colleges." *Journal of College Student Retention Research, Theory, and Practice,* 2001, 3(3), 243–263.

Hagedorn, L. S., Perrakis, A. I., and Maxwell, W. "The Positive Commandments: Ten Ways Community Colleges Help Students Succeed." *Community College Journal,* 2006, 76(5), 58–61.

Hagedorn, L. S., Perrakis, A. I., and Maxwell, W. "The Negative Commandments: Ten Ways Urban Community Colleges Hinder Student Success." *Florida Journal of Educational Administration and Policy,* forthcoming.

Jay, G. M., and D'Augelli, A. R. "Social Support and Adjustment to University Life: A Comparison of African American and White Freshmen." *Journal of Community Psychology,* 1991, *19,* 95–108.

Levin, M., and Levin, J. "A Critical Examination of Academic Retention Programs for At-Risk Minority College Students." *Journal of College Student Development,* 1991, *32,* 323–334.

National Center for Education Statistics. *Fast Facts: Degrees Conferred by Sex and Race.* Washington, D.C.: U.S. Department of Education, 2005.

Pope, M. L. "Meeting the Challenges to African American Men at Community Colleges." In M. C. Cuyjet and Associates (eds.), *African American Men in College.* San Francisco: Jossey-Bass, 2006.

Rendon, L. I., Jalomo, R. E., and Nora, A. "Theoretical Considerations in the Study of Minority Student Retention in Higher Education." In J. Braxton (ed.), *Reworking the Student Departure Puzzle.* Nashville, Tenn.: Vanderbilt University Press, 2000.

ATHENA I. PERRAKIS is assistant professor of leadership studies, chair of the higher education specialization, and director of the Community College Leadership Development Initiatives doctoral fellows program in the School of Leadership and Education Sciences at the University of San Diego.

3

Previous research has neglected to explore identities and development among male students at community colleges. This chapter provides some insight into who these men are, their precollege gender socialization experiences, and conflicts that impede the development of productive masculinities.

Masculinities Go to Community College: Understanding Male Identity Socialization and Gender Role Conflict

Frank Harris III, Shaun R. Harper

"The Case of the Missing Men," a front-page news story in the January 26, 2007, issue of the *Chronicle of Higher Education*, focused on gaps in college enrollments between undergraduate men and women. As is the case with most other treatments of gender in the higher education literature, the story highlighted disparities at four-year institutions, leaving readers relatively uninformed about similar trends at community colleges. Also problematic is the insufficient attention given to gender identity development, as well as attitudinal and behavioral expressions among male community college students. Most of what has been published about men at community colleges pertains to how many enroll and actualize the aspirations with which they entered (completing one course for skill acquisition, earning a certificate or associate degree, or transferring to a four-year institution) and, secondarily, the extent to which they are engaged in educationally purposeful activities. In 2006, men were 41.4 percent of students enrolled at two-year colleges and earned 38.4 percent of associate degrees awarded (U.S. Department of Education, 2007).

Although gendered attainment disparities exist across all racial groups, the gap is widest among black students, with black women earning 68.6 percent of associate degrees. Analyses of data from the Community College Survey of Student Engagement (2006) revealed that women put forth more academic effort and spend more time studying, reading, doing homework,

WILEY InterScience® DISCOVER SOMETHING GREAT

NEW DIRECTIONS FOR COMMUNITY COLLEGES, no. 142, Summer 2008 © 2008 Wiley Periodicals, Inc.
Published online in Wiley InterScience (www.interscience.wiley.com) • DOI: 10.1002/cc.322

and participating in other class-related activities. Furthermore, black male respondents to the survey were less likely than their same-race female counterparts to discuss ideas or readings with others outside class, use the Internet for academic work and research, or spend significant amounts of time studying. Thirty-one percent of black men were uncertain of their plans to return to college the next term, compared to 24 percent of black women. These engagement data, absent of social context to explain gender differences, are hardly useful for educators who endeavor to enhance male student outcomes, increase their participation in enriching educational experiences, and ultimately improve their persistence toward associate degree attainment and transfer rates to four-year institutions.

Disparities in enrollment, attainment, and engagement constitute most of what is known about men at community colleges and therefore make the exploration of gendered questions necessary: What prior gender socialization experiences do men bring with them to college? How do variable masculinities and identity conflicts affect male students' attitudes and behaviors on campus? And what sociocultural factors explain gender differences in engagement and retention within community colleges? These questions have been explored theoretically and empirically using samples of male undergraduates at four-year institutions (Davis, 2002; Harper, 2004; Harper, Harris, and Mmeje, 2005; F. Harris, 2006), but not at community colleges.

Informed by perspectives from sociology, men's studies, and education, this chapter devotes attention to some of the challenges and experiences of men at community colleges. Our exclusive reliance on published literature pertaining to male students at four-year institutions is attributable to the dearth of research exploring men at community colleges. Notwithstanding, we examine how these students are socialized and how various dimensions of their identities intersect, regardless of postsecondary educational context (meaning, two-year or four-year).

Manhood Messages: From Boyhood to College

This section provides insight into the precollege sociocultural factors that contribute to the behavioral trends that are common among male students in college contexts. We consider some of the published literature on boyhood, adolescence, and masculinities. Several socializing agents are identified by researchers as key influences on boys' and young men's precollege gender socialization. Families, male peer groups, and schools are consistently cited as having the most significant and lasting effects on the development of masculine identities for boys (Harper, Harris, and Mmeje, 2005; Kimmel and Messner, 2007; Kimmel, Hearn, and Connell, 2005). These influences are discussed in further detail below.

Parents and Familial Influences. The traditional American family structure facilitates the gender socialization of children (Kimmel and Messner, 2007). This process entails teaching and reinforcing norms and expectations of gendered behavior, which are respectively characterized as masculine and feminine for boys and girls. Children learn the expectations of gender performance for boys and girls (and subsequently men and women) by way of the direct and implicit messages they receive from their parents, as well as through observation and imitation of their parents' gendered behaviors and interactions (MacNaughton, 2006). Children learn throughout their development that domestic duties are culturally associated with women and femininities. Conversely, men and masculinities are associated with duties that represent physical rigor, strength, and power.

The interactions that characterize father-son relationships are especially critical during the process of gender socialization. The ways in which a father shapes his son's gender identity is informed by his own conceptualization of gender. More often than not, fathers' perceptions of masculinities are heavily influenced by traditional, socially constructed expectations. As such, Harper (2004) maintained that "no father wants his son to grow up being a 'pussy,' 'sissy,' 'punk,' or 'softy'—terms commonly associated with boys who fail to live up to the traditional standards of masculinities in America" (p. 92).

Fathers' expectations are reinforced through their daily interactions with their sons and reflected in the toys they purchase, the games they teach their sons, and the strategies they employ for punishing and rewarding gender performance. Fathers are also chiefly responsible for getting their sons involved in sports, martial arts, and other socializing activities that are popular among boys. These activities, coupled with the pressure from fathers to perform gender along stereotypical norms, lead boys to internalize the masculine values of competitiveness, toughness, and aggressiveness. Since these activities and interactions often take place in male-dominated spaces, boys also learn the language and lessons of patriarchy and male privilege (Griffin, 1998).

Male Peer Groups. Male peers also have profound influences on boys' gender identities. Interactions with male peers reinforce the early lessons about gender and masculinities that are learned primarily in the home. Harris (1998) contended that the influence of male peers on gender performance among boys is more intense than parental influences. Similarly, Pollack (2000) described a boy code, which restricts emotional expression among boys. Boys consider being called a "girl," "sissy," or "fag" highly insulting. Therefore, many boys conform to the expectations of their peers by engaging in behaviors and expressing attitudes that are contradictory to what they deem appropriate and desirable in order to avoid these characterizations.

Participating in sports also weighs heavily in peer interactions among boys. Sports provide contexts for boys to establish status by way of physical dominance and competitiveness (Griffin, 1998). Martin and Harris (2006) suggested that boys who can run the fastest, throw the farthest, and hit the hardest are positioned at the top of the hierarchy within their peer groups. Conversely, boys who are not gifted athletically and those who are uncomfortable interacting in male-dominated spaces struggle to gain the acceptance of their peers; they are often the targets of teasing and bullying.

Gilbert and Gilbert (1998) noted that boys' peer interactions are shaped by their athletic prowess in school settings too.

Schools as Venues for Socialization. Masculinizing practices, as characterized by Swain (2005), are heavily situated in traditional American school settings. Gender-related lessons and messages that are consumed by boys in schools are remarkably consistent with those reinforced within families and peer groups. Scholars consistently note that the tasks that lead to academic success do not complement the activities in which boys engage to achieve a masculine identity. Swain described the relationship between achieving a masculine identity and attending to schoolwork as fundamentally incompatible, given the processes of gender socialization for boys. For boys, learning and studying are equated with femininity.

Establishing a masculine identity becomes especially difficult in middle and high school contexts in which sports and heterosexuality emerge as important indicators of masculinities. The most popular boys are those who are perceived to be cool, which is defined in large part by a young man's athleticism and his heterosexual desirability. Teenage boys who establish reputations for engaging in sexual relationships with girls are considered among the coolest by their peers (Davis and Jordan, 1994). Thus, increasing their popularity and masculine statuses becomes an incentive for boys to pursue sex with girls and share the details of these acts with their peers. Consequently sex and girls are often the subjects of highly charged sexist behaviors and conversations among male teens. There is intense pressure to engage in these conversations; those who choose not to do so are viewed with suspicion by peers.

The patterns of interactions among middle and high school boys also persist into postsecondary settings. Ludeman (2004) asserted, "If the male socialization process indeed shapes or restricts the emotional skills and development of boys and men, then it seems likely that the demands of the college environment will create challenges for men related to their relationships and experiences on the college campus" (pp. 79–80). Ludeman's remarks facilitate our transition to the next section of this chapter, which considers the ways in which traditional patterns of male socialization conflict with men's development and success in college.

Masculinities in Conflict During College

Scholars who have explored undergraduate men in their research have not focused their analyses on men enrolled at community colleges. Therefore, little is known about the gender-related developmental challenges with which these men must contend. This discussion of masculinities in conflict during college is, by default, informed by the published research on college men who attend four-year institutions.

Higher education researchers have linked healthy psychosocial development with the achievement of important outcomes in college (Chickering and Reisser, 1993; Evans, Forney, and Guido-DiBrito, 1998). Engaging in campus activities and organizations, cultivating meaningful friendships and interpersonal relationships, and seeking help when necessary are some indicators of healthy psychosocial development for college students. College men are often reluctant to exhibit these behaviors because they are traditionally defined as feminine and conflict with lessons learned about masculinity prior to college (Harper, Harris, and Mmeje, 2005; Ludeman, 2004). Moreover, men's adherence to unproductive masculine conceptions such as sexism, homophobia, violence, and anti-intellectualism are often requisite for their access to male peer groups. As is the case in high school, men who openly reject these conceptions risk being alienated or having their masculinities questioned by their male peers (Kimmel, 1996; Messner, 2001). When examined critically, the incongruence between the behaviors that are linked empirically to student development and success in college and those that constitute the performance of traditional masculinities are evident.

Male Gender Role Conflict

Male gender role conflict (MGRC) is an empirically grounded phenomenon that helps to make sense of the gender and identity-related challenges with which college men must contend. O'Neil (1981) characterized MGRC as a negative consequence of the discrepancies between men's authentic selves and the idealized, socially constructed images that are culturally associated with masculinity. When men are unable to perform masculinity, they are likely to view themselves as less masculine and assume others will do the same. MGRC is also directly related to men's fears of being perceived as feminine (O'Neil, 1981). Femininity, when exhibited by men, is associated with being gay and therefore encourages homophobia and hypermasculinity among men. Young men are socialized at very early ages to strategically avoid values, attitudes, and behaviors that are socially constructed as feminine or gay. Thus, the detrimental effects of MGRC are not surprising.

The consequences of MGRC on development and outcomes for college men are noteworthy. Several behavioral patterns that are associated with MGRC are reportedly prevalent among men in college. Restricted emotionality relates to men's difficulty or unwillingness to express their feelings, their refusal to display emotional vulnerability, and their disdain for male femininity. This pattern stems from the belief that disclosing feelings, emotions, and vulnerabilities is an indication of weakness and therefore should not be exhibited by men (O'Neil, 1981). Seeking help through counseling and other means of emotional expressiveness is also inconsistent with restricted emotionality. In college contexts, men who have internalized restricted emotionality can be overwhelmed by failure, setbacks, and frustrations (O'Neil, 1981). Once internalized, these feelings surface through acts of aggressiveness and, in extreme cases, physical violence. O'Neil also found that restricted emotionality discourages genuine interpersonal closeness between men. This may explain why college men often limit their interactions with male peers to stereotypically masculine norms (Ludeman, 2004).

Socialized control, power, and competition is a second pattern of MGRC that informs this discussion of college men. Whereas restricted emotionality denotes men's control over their feelings and emotions, this pattern relates to men's desires to regulate the situations and the people in their lives (O'Neil, 1981). The pattern describes a man's tendencies to compete with and show superiority over other men in order to assert his masculinities. Key sites for power and competition among college men are sexual relationships with women, status within exclusively male peer groups, and the accumulation of material possessions. When college men are unsuccessful in securing the power and control within these and similar contexts, they often rely on other, usually destructive, strategies for doing so. For instance, O'Neil (1981) posited that socialized power and control are achieved through homophobia within male peer groups. "Homophobia," O'Neil writes, "is a device of social control to maintain traditional male behavior appropriate to social situations and to control all men, not just [gay men]" (p. 208).

Finally, men's obsession with achievement and success has also been identified as a behavioral pattern of MGRC that provides insight into behaviors and outcomes for college men. Men are socialized to embrace the breadwinner role in the home. Thus, many college men pursue postsecondary degrees for access to high-paying jobs and careers, and thereby facilitate their fulfillment of this expectation. This pattern also partially explains why men have traditionally been overrepresented among students pursuing degrees in business, engineering, and other technical disciplines. Fears of failure and intense pressure to succeed are two consequences accompanying men's obsession with achievement and success (O'Neil, 1981). College men who fall into this behavioral pattern are predisposed to physical and emotional stress and reliance on food, alcohol, and drugs to sooth anxieties.

Identity Conflicts Among Four Community College Male Students

In this section, we present the profiles of four racially different men enrolled in community colleges. Each student is confronting a unique set of challenges relating to his masculine identity. These profiles illustrate the concepts and conflicts discussed in the chapter.

The Working White Mechanic. Adam came from a working-class background. While pursuing an associate degree in business, he simultaneously worked part time as a mechanic in order to make ends meet. Adam was a former high school all-American football player. In fact, he had expected to earn an athletic scholarship to attend a major university with a high-profile football program, but in the summer prior to his senior year of high school, he was in a motorcycle accident and suffered severe head and leg injuries, which ended his athletic career. The accident and subsequent injuries left Adam angry and depressed, and they marked the beginning of a downward spiral.

Adam did not have grades and test scores that would earn him admission to a four-year institution without an athletic scholarship. Therefore, he pursued other career options that did not require a degree. To cope, he began abusing alcohol, having risky sex (which led him to fatherhood at age nineteen), and occasionally engaging in violent altercations with others. In his third semester of community college, Adam encountered a host of challenges. He struggled academically and found it difficult to fit in with the "smart kids," as he often referred to his classmates. His girlfriend suggested that he talk with his professors, join a study group, or consult a tutor at the college's academic support center. Adam refused for fear that his classmates and professor would view him as incapable. "They already think I'm stupid and don't belong there. I am not going to kiss their asses to pass a class!" he exclaimed.

Adam also found it difficult to accept the opportunity costs he had to endure in order to attend college. Prior to enrolling, he worked sixty hours a week and earned enough income to allow his girlfriend to stay at home and take care of their two children. Suddenly Adam had to reduce his work hours by half to make time for classes and studying. Consequently, his girlfriend took a part-time job to supplement their income. Adam recently asked a friend, "What kind of man has two kids and quits working so he can go and read poetry at some damn college?"

The Struggling Asian Help Seeker. Jimmy grew up in a traditional Vietnamese family in which education and high academic achievement were constantly emphasized. He has two older brothers, both of whom graduated with honors from top universities. His issues stemmed primarily from the pressure he felt to follow his father's professional footsteps. Jimmy's father expected him to earn an accounting degree and assume ownership of the family business. But Jimmy wanted to be a writer, which had become a source of tension between him and his father.

In his second semester of college, Jimmy began to struggle academically and suffered from undiagnosed depression. He also had not established any meaningful friendships in college, in sharp contrast to his high school years when he was highly engaged in clubs and regularly enjoyed social interactions with his friends. An academic adviser offered access to tutors, counseling, and other sources of support, and she encouraged him to consider changing his major. However, Jimmy refused to take advantage of these options, fearing they would be met with his father's disapproval.

The Latino Homeboy. Erik had always enjoyed school and was a good student until his freshman year of high school, when he began hanging out with a group of young men who had a bad influence on him. They regularly skipped school, spent significant amounts of time pursuing sex with girls, and were occasionally involved in minor illegal activities. At times Erik tried to pull away from the group and get on the right path. However, the other questioned his loyalty and manhood. Somehow Erik managed to complete high school, but he decided not to participate in graduation for fear of his friends' reaction. In fact, one year had passed before Erik disclosed to them that he earned his high school diploma.

A critical moment occurred in Erik's life that motivated him to reconsider his future and recapture some of his promise and potential: his father became terminally ill. Realizing that in his father's absence he would need to care for his mother and two young sisters, Erik decided to enroll in community college to pursue a vocational certificate and an associate degree. His friends from high school offered a perspective on his decision: "School is for girls and sissies. If you need to support your family, be a man and go out and get a real job." Despite this advice, he lived at home with his mother and siblings, commuted to campus each day, and decided not to work so he could concentrate on school. Erik's performance in college classes was satisfactory; however, he often questioned his decision to return to school and wondered if he should have gotten a full-time job.

The Closeted Black Gay Achiever. Toreé graduated from high school with an academic record that would have easily gained him admission to a four-year institution. He chose to spend his first two years at a community college to relieve his family of some of the financial burden of paying for college. Toreé came from a tightly knit family with strong religious values. In fact, his closest male friends were those he had met in church as a youngster. The significant roles that family and religion played in Toreé's life and identity were profound.

During his time in community college, Toreé established a reputation as an outstanding student and a respected campus leader. He served as president of the student government and was well known by many of his peers. On the surface, he appeared to be enjoying a healthy and fulfilling college student experience. However, no one around him knew that Toreé was incredibly conflicted. As a junior in high school, Toreé discovered his attraction to other men and started engaging in sexual experiences and relationships with boyfriends. Toreé worried that disclosing his sexual orientation would change the way he was perceived on campus. Moreover, he was certain that his family would disown him if they learned he was gay. Over the years, he had heard his father make strong homophobic remarks about gay and lesbian persons. Also, given his religious background, Toreé was concerned that his sexual orientation would bring shame to his family. Overcommitment was a strategy he employed to cope with the stress and anxiety. The community college had only a handful of student clubs, and Toreé was involved in nearly all of them. Of course, he was applauded for his high level of service and commitment. But in spite the success and status he enjoyed in college, Toreé became increasingly depressed and unhappy.

A Conclusion on Conflict Among Community College Men

Though racially different, Adam, Jimmy, Erik, and Toreé, had one thing in common: each experienced conflicts related to his masculine identity while enrolled in community college. These four men's stories are more common than atypical, which makes understanding the unique issues and gendered experiences of college men urgently important. For example, two gender-related challenges were prominent in Adam's profile. First, he had clearly internalized the breadwinner role that men are often socialized to embrace. He viewed his decision to enroll in community college as a violation of this prevalent masculine norm, especially considering that his girlfriend had to share the responsibility of earning the income necessary to provide for their family. Second, much of the success Adam experienced during his adolescent years came by way of his participation in sports. Thus, returning to school required him to learn new skills and develop his intellectual competence. These new growth and learning processes resulted in increased anxiety, feelings of inadequacy, and frustration.

Taken as a whole, Adam's behaviors were consistent with the restricted emotionality and socialized power and control patterns of MGRC. Sources of support that validated his new identity as a student would have eased his college transition. Also, connecting Adam with a male faculty or staff mentor could have been helpful. Supporting Adam through his challenges may have provided an opportunity to identify other men on campus who had recently returned to school and were balancing academic demands with caring for their families and working off campus. Finally, Adam may have benefited from career advising. Given his past involvement and success in athletics, pursuing a career in coaching, athletics administration, sports medicine, or a related field may have elicited more enthusiasm for college. Getting reconnected to sports also could have offered therapeutic benefits for Adam by providing some closure on the unexpected termination of his football career. Similarly thoughtful approaches should be used to understand and help resolve identity conflicts with students like Jimmy, Erik, Toreé, and other men with conflicted identities at community colleges. We offer the following potentially promising suggestions:

- Encourage male students to reconsider their negative perceptions of help seeking that many have been socialized to assume
- Provide opportunities for critical reflection on masculinity through journaling, course readings, analyzing popular media, and other assignments (Davis and Laker, 2004)
- Increase male students' participation in campus activities and programs that facilitate healthy identity development and lead to productive outcomes
- Provide opportunities for bonding by way of facilitated discussion groups and other activities that are popular among male students

- Collect campus-level data (interviews, focus groups, and surveys for example) from male students to assess their gender-specific needs
- Organize a committee of student affairs administrators, counselors, faculty members, coaches, and student leaders to provide proactive campuswide leadership in addressing issues concerning male students

One question remains: How do masculinities in community college contexts differ from those in four-year institutions? The paucity of published literature that provides insight into the gender-related experiences of community college men makes this question difficult to answer. While this chapter serves as a first step toward understanding community college men, additional inquiries that consider their unique challenges and experiences are urgently necessary. Studies that provide insight into the ways in which community college campus contexts both facilitate and hinder gender identity development for male students are especially needed.

References

"The Case of the Missing Men." *Chronicle of Higher Education,* Jan. 26, 2007, p. A1.

Chickering, A. W., and Reisser, L. *Education and Identity.* (2nd ed.) San Francisco: Jossey-Bass, 1993.

Community College Survey of Student Engagement. *Act on Fact: Using Data to Improve Student Success, 2006 Findings.* Austin: University of Texas, 2006.

Davis, J. E., and Jordan, W. J. "The Effects of School Context, Structure, and Experience on African American Males in Middle and High School." *Journal of Negro Education,* 1994, *63,* 570–587.

Davis, T. "Voices of Gender Role Conflict: The Social Construction of College Men's Identity." *Journal of College Student Development,* 2002, *43*(4), 508–521.

Davis, T., and Laker, J. "Connecting Men to Academic and Student Affairs Programs and Services." In G. Kellom (ed.), *Developing Effective Programs and Services for College Men.* New Directions for Student Services, no. 107. San Francisco: Jossey-Bass, 2004.

Evans, N. J., Forney, D. S., and Guido-DiBrito, F. *Student Development in College: Theory, Research, and Practice.* San Francisco: Jossey-Bass, 1998.

Gilbert, R., and Gilbert, P. *Masculinity Goes to School.* New York: Routledge, 1998.

Griffin, P. *Strong Women, Deep Closets: Lesbians and Homophobia in Sports.* Champaign, Ill.: Human Kinetics, 1998.

Harper, S. R. "The Measure of a Man: Conceptualizations of Masculinity Among High-Achieving African American Male College Students." *Berkeley Journal of Sociology,* 2004, *48*(1), 89–107.

Harper, S. R., Harris III, F., and Mmeje, K. "A Theoretical Model to Explain the Overrepresentation of College Men Among Campus Judicial Offenders: Implications for Campus Administrators." *NASPA Journal,* 2005, *42*(4), 565–588.

Harris III, F. "The Role of Pre-College Socialization in the Meanings College Men Make of Masculinities." Paper presented at the Association for the Study of Higher Education annual meeting, Anaheim, Calif., Nov. 2006.

Harris, J. R. *The Nature Assumption: Why Children Turn Out the Way They Do.* London: Bloomsbury, 1998.

Kimmel, M. S. *Manhood in America: A Cultural History.* New York: Free Press, 1996.

Kimmel, M. S., Hearn, J., and Connell, R. W. (eds.). *Handbook of Studies on Men and Masculinities.* Thousand Oaks, Calif.: Sage, 2005.

Kimmel, M. S., and Messner, M. A. (eds.). *Men's Lives.* (7th ed.) Needham Heights, Mass.: Allyn and Bacon, 2007.
Ludeman, R. B. "Arrested Emotional Development: Connecting College Men, Emotions, and Misconduct." In G. Kellom (ed.), *Developing Effective Programs and Services for College Men.* New Directions for Student Services, no. 107. San Francisco: Jossey-Bass, 2004.
MacNaughton, G. "Constructing Gender in Early-Years Education." In C. Skelton, B. Francis, and L. Smulyan (eds.), *The Sage Handbook of Gender and Education.* Thousand Oaks, Calif.: Sage, 2006.
Martin, B. E., and Harris III, F. "Examining Productive Conceptions of Masculinities: Lessons Learned from Academically Driven African American Male Student-Athletes." *Journal of Men's Studies,* 2006, *14*(3), 359–378.
Messner, M. A. "Friendship, Intimacy, and Sexuality." In S. M. Whitehead and F. J. Barrett (eds.), *The Masculinities Reader.* Malden, Mass.: Blackwell, 2001.
O'Neil, J. M. "Patterns of Gender Role Conflict and Strain: Sexism and Fear of Femininity in Men's Lives." *Personnel and Guidance Journal,* 1981, *60,* 203–210.
Pollack, W. S. *Real Boys' Voices.* New York: Random House, 2000.
Swain, J. "Masculinities in Education." In M. Kimmel, J. Hearn, and R. W. Connell (eds.), *Handbook of Studies on Men and Masculinities.* Thousand Oaks, Calif.: Sage, 2005.
U.S. Department of Education. *Digest of Education Statistics, 2006.* Washington, D.C.: National Center for Education Statistics, 2007.

FRANK HARRIS III is assistant professor of postsecondary education at San Diego State University.

SHAUN R. HARPER is assistant professor of higher education management at the University of Pennsylvania Graduate School of Education.

4

This chapter presents findings from interviews with female community college students in science, technology, engineering, and mathematics fields regarding their learning experiences, interaction with faculty, and educational and career aspirations.

Broadening Female Participation in Science, Technology, Engineering, and Mathematics: Experiences at Community Colleges

Soko S. Starobin, Frankie Santos Laanan

Over the past few decades, community colleges have helped increase the representation of female and minority students in the fields of science, technology, engineering, and mathematics (Brazziel and Brazziel, 1994; Starobin, 2004; Starobin and Laanan, 2005). These institutions provide educational and vocational opportunities for students through technical education, academic transfer to four-year colleges and universities, remedial, continuing education, and community service (Cohen and Brawer, 2003; Laanan, 2003). The nation's community colleges enroll over 10 million credit and noncredit students, which include more than 57 percent of female students and 38 percent of minority students in the student population pool (National Center for Education Statistics, 2003). Given a substantial percentage of racial and ethnic minorities and women enrolled in community colleges, this pool of individuals serves as a potential group to fulfill the nation's science, technology, engineering, and mathematics (STEM) workforce needs.

Federal Initiatives for Broadening Participation

Federal agencies, such as the National Science Board (2003) and the National Academy of Engineering (2005), have recognized the role of community colleges in increasing workforce competency. The global market has

WILEY InterScience® DISCOVER SOMETHING GREAT

NEW DIRECTIONS FOR COMMUNITY COLLEGES, no. 142, Summer 2008 © 2008 Wiley Periodicals, Inc.
Published online in Wiley InterScience (www.interscience.wiley.com) • DOI: 10.1002/cc.323

shifted from a demand for low-wage, low-skilled workers to a need for high-tech, high-skilled occupations. Community colleges have and will continue to provide opportunities for citizens to acquire new skills and become technologically competent through career and technical education programs and STEM education. The National Science Foundation (NSF) has played an important role as well through increasing funding directly to community colleges, from approximately $7 million in 1993 to over $35 million in 1999 (National Science Foundation, 2001). NSF-funded programs such as STEM Talent Expansion Programs (STEP) and Advanced Technological Education (ATE) Programs specifically support implementation strategies that have led to an increase in the number of community college students studying in STEM, transferring to four-year institutions, and graduating with a STEM baccalaureate degree. These programs are strongly encouraged to develop support services and programs that increase participation among traditionally underrepresented student populations: low income, ethnic and racial minorities, persons with disabilities, and women. One of the purposes of ATE programs is to "improve the educational opportunities of postsecondary students by creating comprehensive articulation partnerships between 2-year and 4-year institutions" (National Science Foundation, 2001, p. 1).

Transfer Function in Community Colleges in STEM Education

Community colleges serve as a stepping-stone for underrepresented groups that otherwise never thought of studying or pursuing STEM-related fields (Laanan, 2001; Starobin, 2004). In a study using the 2001 National Survey of Recent College Graduates, Tsapogas (2004) found that more than 40 percent of science and engineering bachelor's and master's graduates attended community colleges at some point in their educational paths. These graduates were more likely to be Hispanic, African American, American Indian, or Alaskan native; older than traditional-age students; and with parents with lower educational attainment. Tsapogas also found that female science and engineering students are more likely than male graduates to have attended community college, especially among graduates who are married and have children in the household. Tsapogas concluded that community colleges are important institutions in the educational lives of science and engineering graduates. Flexible schedules, low tuition, proximity to jobs, and open access admissions make community colleges attractive to a diverse student body, especially female graduates "who are attempting to manage families, education, and sometimes, jobs" (p. 6).

To date, little research has focused on women enrolled in community colleges and their decision to pursue a STEM baccalaureate degree (Starobin and Laanan, 2005). A study conducted by Starobin (2004) argues that receiving encouragement from individuals at home and school helps female students in STEM programs develop their self-concept. These individuals can be faculty, counselors, advisers, friends, and family members. Starobin (2004) also identified a need for additional studies to examine female students in STEM at community colleges by applying qualitative research inquiry. To fulfill the void in the literature, this chapter presents findings from interviews with female community college students in STEM fields regarding their learning experiences, interaction with faculty, and educational and career aspirations. It also discusses implications for practice and policy to facilitate female participation in STEM.

Exemplary Practices: Two Tales

The study examined here reports on the second-year efforts of a dissemination project to increase participation among female students in STEM fields. The project was designed to develop media presentations that educate the public and college students about the pathway to a STEM baccalaureate degree, create a STEM transfer guide for prospective students attending two-year colleges, and build a Web site for academic counselors, transfer center coordinators, students in two-year colleges, business and industry, researchers, policymakers, and the public.

To achieve the study objectives, the project investigators identified and then studied exemplary transfer programs that increase participation among female and minority students in STEM. Thus, the purposes of this study were to understand how gender influenced learning experiences among female students in a preengineering program at a community college; provide students the opportunity to reflect on and share their academic and personal experiences; and identify factors that help female students transfer from a community college to a four-year university in engineering.

Guided group interviews were conducted at Highline Community College (HCC) and Seattle Central Community College (SCCC), both part of the Northwest Engineering Talent Expansion Partnership (NW-ETEP), which provides an opportunity for every student who is motivated and prepared to earn an engineering degree in Washington State. One of the objectives of the NW-ETEP is to increase the number of women who earn engineering degrees by providing support programs. Components of this program include a comprehensive team comprising community college faculty and student services providers; an on-site community college coordinator; and academic support, major and career exploration, and transfer assistance.

Highline Community College. The main HCC campus is located twenty minutes south of downtown Seattle. HCC, which enrolled approximately fifteen thousand students in 2005–2006, is one of the state's largest postsecondary institutions. It offers associate degrees that provide preparation for transfer to four-year institutions along with associate of applied science degrees and certificate programs. More than 40 percent of students indicate that their intent is to transfer to four-year institutions. With regard to student demographics at HCC, more than 60 percent of the students are female, and approximately 50 percent are ethnic minority. As a result of the NW-ETEP initiative, HCC provides academic and support services developed by the on-site coordinator and faculty members. HCC also has dedicated classroom space for NW-ETEP participants for academic and social activities.

Seattle Central Community College. Located in the vibrant Broadway Street area, Seattle Central Community College (SCCC) enrolled more than seventeen thousand students during the 2005–2006 academic year. Students at SCCC are significantly more diverse than the city of Seattle: 40 percent are ethnic minorities, and 56.5 percent are female. SCCC emphasizes preparation of students to transfer to a four-year institution by providing well-articulated associate degrees, such as associate of art, associate of science, and associate of applied science-transfer degrees. NW-ETEP participants at SCCC can receive academic and social support from the on-site coordinator at the College Transfer Center as well as from faculty members.

Reflections and Experiences of Female STEM Students

The guided group interviews consisted of three female students who were invited by faculty and program coordinators of NW-ETEP programs at HCC and SCCC. The researchers requested that the program coordinators invite female engineering students who are planning to transfer to a four-year institution. Female facilitators guided group interviews to create a safe and comfortable space for the participants to express their opinions. The questions that guided the interviews addressed such topics as individuals who contributed to the students' choice to pursue an engineering degree, programs and services at the community college that helped students prepare for transfer and make career decisions, and academic environments that made students comfortable and uncomfortable. Data from the interviews were tape-recorded and transcribed. The researchers reviewed and coded the transcripts to identify recurring themes and opinions.

In the following section, highlights of the guided group interviews are presented to capture female students' self-expressions and reflections with regard to their personal and academic experiences.

Wish I Knew Before. A lack of social and academic support for female students to pursue STEM fields can impede their academic and career aspirations (Starobin and Laanan, 2005). Female students also tend to believe in the long-standing stereotype that men are good in math and women are stronger in humanities (Seymour and Hewitt, 1997). Many of the participants of the group interviews said they wished someone had told them earlier that they could study engineering:

> Nobody had ever suggested or even put the thought in my mind that I could actually do something that big, that grand, and so after investigating it I thought, Oh, okay, might as well. So, that is how I got into engineering. I sure wish someone had said something when I was younger because being older

> it is harder. I just missed so much, you know, I think if I had been encouraged when I was younger. [Lori]

> I wish somebody had told me about it [engineering] earlier. Until I took physics I did not know, you know, I did not know engineers existed. I did not know who designed those buildings. . . . I think if somebody had communicated to me personally in middle school in one of my math classes or science classes, I think I would have probably been thinking about it [engineering] a lot earlier. [Eleena]

> For me, it was my dad. He was always a good example, but I never thought I was good enough with math to become an engineer, so for years and years, I decided not to do it. I talked to my teacher who was Rebecca, and she was actually very encouraging that if I just stuck with it, I would probably do pretty good. [Celeste]

It is noteworthy that these students never mentioned that they did not like or have a fear of studying math or science. Furthermore, most of them had some positive experiences in studying math and science in middle school. Their comments affirm that a lack of support, encouragement, and reinforcement harms females' intent to study engineering. One female student passionately claimed, "I just wish someone had planted the seed and mentioned that you know, engineering is possible, and you can do this . . . just that little statement just like changed my world basically."

All of these comments also confirm that these students vividly remembered that moment when a faculty member or counselor told them that they could study engineering and become an engineer. Such positive personal encounters and communication with faculty and counselors consistently emerge as a vital element for success among female students in engineering.

See a Clear Pathway. Almost all participants agreed that advising from faculty and program coordinators was critical in the decision to continue their engineering study and pursue transfer to a four-year institution. Some were quite surprised by the support that they received from their faculty. At HCC, students who are enrolled in Engineering 101 learned about required courses for transfer, financial aid, and support services available for them. During the course, students develop a two-year plan to map an academic path to transfer. When students were asked about programs and services that helped them to prepare for transfer, Lori responded, "Without the two-year plan I would be one of those perpetual students because I always like to add an art class each quarter, and take a Web design class this quarter but the two-year plan keeps me focused. . . . . The two-year plan saved me with financial aid, too. "

Without a clear understanding and guidance, it is difficult to stay focused and not get behind in the rigorous courses typical of engineering programs. Another student agreed: "Having things planned out for the right quarters, you can get things done on time." In addition, students begin to develop skills to survive challenging courses and sustain good grades. One student, Erin, said, "You can also look at and determine which classes you take when and how best to break it up like as far as, Okay, do I want to take chemistry, or do I want to take physics, or do I want to take an elective here?"

Seeing a clear pathway to transfer can be critical for female students. Once they learn not to be preoccupied with or afraid of their immediate challenges, they begin to apply the same principle to their content learning. Erin said, "I love that as well seeing all the little dots connected, seeing how things relate to everything, being able to take something from calculus class and throw it into my engineering classes and come out with something that works, it is very cool."

It is evident that content learning also serves as a contributing factor in their persistence.

Leadership Grows in a Unique Community. One of the most significant findings in this study was that community colleges provide a unique learning culture and environment for female students in engineering. Interestingly, a plethora of literature documents the negative learning culture and environment at four-year research institutions for female students in STEM fields (Lovitts, 2001; Sax, 1994; Seymour and Hewitt, 1997). However, when students were asked to reflect on their gender-conscious opinions on the learning environment at their community college, their responses portray the unique culture and environment that the college creates, which appears as a contrast to the culture and environment of four-year institutions found in past studies:

> You know, we have all different people from all around the world here, and it is just such a global community. [Brittney]

Unlike the traditional STEM academic culture that four-year research institutions create, the learning environment at a community college directly reflects the community with regard to political orientations, diversity, and lifestyle. Such a diverse culture at the community college may help female students focus on their engineering studies rather than being conscious of their gender. These students say that once they get to know their classmates, regardless of their gender, they feel comfortable in their science and engineering classes. One student, Patricia, described how she sees herself in such surroundings: "For me, I almost always end up managing the project. I feel like the mommy a lot, so we have always split up pretty equally [between males and females]. Like I have had the same group in statics and dynamics—we meet, and I always make sure they are doing their part, and they are coming to the meetings, and they know what they are doing. So, I feel more like the manager of the group."

At HCC, engineering students participate in the annual human-powered paper vehicle competition: they are required to design, develop, and construct a vehicle that is made out of 90 percent paper and 10 percent other materials and powered by a human. Erin reflected on the experiences in the project: "I am glad that I finished that [competition] because it just was so awesome to go there and have it work. May and I, the other girl on the team, really bonded because we had to fight through this thing, and it really made me step up and be a leader. Before that I was kinda like just going along with them [males] and doing what they wanted and stuff like that."

Such a unique learning culture and environment encourages female students to do well in the classroom and play a leadership role in classroom activities and assignments. Many female students were surprised to realize they had an ability to lead a group and project among their male classmates. And those who took a risk of becoming a leader began to develop confidence and self-esteem.

Believing Becomes Persistence. With a sense of confidence and self-esteem, female students in the group interviews described their attitudes toward advanced math courses and readiness for transfer to a four-year institution. They wanted other female students to know about their experiences:

> If engineering is something that you want to do, you can just work hard. Everyone works hard. It does not matter if it comes to you more easily than other people. . . it is training. I mean you are not born a fast runner or good athlete. That is something you work on to do. If you want it, go for it. [Celeste]

> It does not matter if you are not so good in math; you can get better, you can practice, talk to people. And study groups are huge, very important, very important. [Erin]

> Scary subject [math], but it is like any other skill. You just have to, you have to learn it. . . . I mean like writing, some people can write books and novels, and I can't. You know, it is a skill that you have to learn. [Lori]

These comments indicate that the female students' attitudes toward advanced math courses are positive. Most important, many of them take the responsibility to work hard and do well. None felt they were less capable of learning advanced math than their male counterparts. Confidence and self-esteem clearly can be cited as an outcome of the NW-ETEP program for these students as they prepare for transfer to an engineering program at a four-year institution:

> I feel like I can go on to the university. I feel like I can do it because I have gone through you know, so many different opportunities that have helped my mentality, just changing that way here at Highline. [Eleena]

> I am a little scared honestly because it is going to be such a big step. It is such a transition, but I think I am going to go in there, and I am gonna hold my own. And I am gonna do well, I am gonna do good things, definitely. [Erin]

As these female students conveyed their confidence and readiness to transfer from a community college to a four-year institution, the positive outcomes of the NW-ETEP program were confirmed. NW-ETEP successfully fostered these students' confidence and academic excellence in preparation for transfer. The researchers were convinced that with the support of the team faculty, student services providers, and an on-site coordinator, these female students have been empowered to thrive and pursue their aspirations to obtain a baccalaureate degree in engineering.

Implications for Practice, Policy, and Future Directions

This investigation pointed out several implications for practice for those interested in creating a learning environment that helps female students as they pursue preengineering programs.

Build a Supportive Environment with Key Constituents. According to most of our female participants, it is critical to find faculty, advisers, or counselors to provide guidance, support, and encouragement at an early stage and throughout their program of study. These key constituents offer critical support to female students as they build their skills and confidence toward successful transfer. Students also find support in fellow students. Community colleges can therefore provide assistance and opportunity for students to build their learning community. The curriculum can be arranged to encourage students to take courses in a sequence so they can build an academic community that supports and nurtures their success. Students often noted the importance of study groups to their academic success. Building the academic community as well as study groups is particularly important for community college female students who have jobs, family responsibilities, and other challenges. Most important, key constituents who help female students are often found in strong academic community and study groups.

Show a Clear Pathway to a Baccalaureate Degree. An introductory course such as Engineering 101 at HCC provides students with the information, skills, and resources they need to navigate the transfer system, course requirements, financial aid, and other factors that lead to successful transfer. To deliver such practices, institutions and programs must value and recognize this curricular content and commit resources to its development and delivery. Once students understand how to navigate their pathway to a baccalaureate degree, they begin to feel comfortable with and confident in overcoming their personal and academic challenges. The group interview participants said that it is critical for female students to believe that they can meet academic challenges. Their positive attitudes toward advanced courses lead to self-confidence and self-esteem.

Send Positive Messages Early. Virtually all students in this study mentioned the importance of faculty and counselors who encouraged them to pursue engineering. Most did not receive these messages at home and wished someone had influenced them sooner. The message they need to receive is simple: "You can do it."

A striking finding from this study was that the majority of the group interview participants wished someone had told them earlier that they could study engineering. To create opportunities for community college female students to receive positive messages, the colleges can partner with four-year institutions to develop a bridge program or summer research program for female students so they can experience the academic environment at a four-year institution. In addition, community colleges can arrange mentoring programs in business and industry for female students to meet female engineers and learn about their career opportunities.

Conclusion

This study provides policy implications for increasing the number of female STEM baccalaureates and beyond. At the National Science Board Workshop, policymakers were encouraged to understand the enormous range of pathways that students take between community colleges and four-year institutions. Furthermore, the National Academy of Engineering urges that "four year schools should accept the responsibility of working with local community colleges to achieve workable articulation with their 2-year engineering programs" (2005, p. 2).

Community colleges as well as their partner four-year institutions are encouraged to seek financial assistance from foundations or agencies such as the National Science Foundation to develop and deliver programs and services to encourage female students to pursue studies in STEM fields. Key to the success of these programs is an on-site coordinator who serves as the conduit and facilitator of the program and its students, faculty, staff, and partners. Resources obtained through such initiatives allow community colleges to develop partnerships not only with four-year institutions for transfer opportunities but with business and industry for students who seek career opportunities. Community colleges can also develop partnerships with K–12 schools to encourage young girls to pursue their studies in STEM fields.

The female students in the group interviews clearly noted the need for both two-year and four-year institutions to strengthen partnerships so that programs and services can be developed to offer positive learning experiences and increase the participation among female students in STEM fields to obtain a baccalaureate degree.

References

Brazziel, W. F., and Brazziel, M. E. "Minority Science and Engineering Doctorate Recipients with Junior and Community College Backgrounds." *Community College Journal of Research and Practice,* 1994, *18*(1), 71–80.

Cohen, A. M., and Brawer, F. B. *The American Community College.* (4th ed.) San Francisco: Jossey-Bass, 2003.

Laanan, F. S. "Transfer Student Adjustment." In F. S. Laanan (ed.), *Transfer Students: Trends and Issues.* New Directions for Community Colleges, no. 114. San Francisco: Jossey-Bass, 2001.

Laanan, F. S. "Degree Aspirations of Two-Year College Students." *Community College of Research and Practice,* 2003, *27,* 495–518.

Lovitts, E. B. *Leaving the Ivory Tower: The Cases and Consequences of Departure from Doctoral Study.* Lanham, Md.: Rowman and Littlefield, 2001.

National Academy of Engineering. *Educating the Engineer of 2020: Adapting Engineering Education to the New Century.* Washington, D.C.: National Academies Press, 2005.

National Center for Education Statistics. *Digest of Education Statistics: 2002.* Washington, D.C.: U.S. Department of Education, 2003.

National Science Board. *The Science and Engineering Workforce Realizing America's Potential.* Washington, D.C.: National Science Foundation, 2003.

National Science Foundation. *National Science Foundation Support for Two-Year Colleges, Fiscal Years 1997–1999: A Report of the Division of Undergraduate Education.* Washington, D.C.: National Science Foundation, 2001.

Sax, L. J. "Predicting Gender and Major Field Differences in Mathematical Self-Concept During College." *Journal of Women and Minorities in Science and Engineering,* 1994, *1*(4), 291–307.

Seymour, E., and Hewitt, N. M. *Talking about Leaving: Why Undergraduates Leave the Sciences.* Boulder, Colo.: Westview, 1997.

Starobin, S. S. "Gender Differences in College Choice, Aspirations, and Self-Concept Among Community College Students in Science, Mathematics, and Engineering." Unpublished doctoral dissertation, University of North Texas, 2004.

Starobin, S. S., and Laanan, F. S. "Influence of Pre-College Experience on Self-Concept Among Community College Students in Science, Mathematics, and Engineering." *Journal of Women and Minorities in Science and Engineering,* 2005, *11*(3), 209–230.

Tsapogas, J. *The Role of Community Colleges in the Education of Recent Science and Engineering Graduates.* Washington, D.C.: National Science Foundation, 2004.

SOKO S. STAROBIN is a clinician faculty member in the department of educational leadership and policy studies at Iowa State University in Ames, Iowa.

FRANKIE SANTOS LAANAN is associate professor in the department of educational leadership and policy studies at Iowa State University in Ames, Iowa.

5

This chapter presents findings from a study of noninstructional community college staff, focusing on staff perception of organizational climate, the impact of gender on staff interactions with faculty and students, and perceptions of workplace satisfaction.

Noninstructional Staff Perceptions of the College Climate

Molly H. Duggan

As of fall 2003, 45 percent of community college employees were termed noninstructional staff, defined as those who perform a variety of tasks on the campus but do not teach. Of this group, over 63 percent were women serving in positions ranging from maintenance to clerks to counselors to presidents (National Center for Education Statistics, 2005). Noninstructional staff are a diverse group; some work behind the scenes keeping the college running smoothly, while others serve in more prominent positions. In many instances, students spend as much time interacting with noninstructional staff as they do with teaching faculty. Despite serving the community college, and its faculty and students, nonteaching staff are often marginalized, their experiences and input frequently discounted. This population, however, is anything but unimportant to the community college; they are part of the very fabric of college. Exploring noninstructional staff perspectives of the college is vital to understanding the organization and effecting change.

Research connects organizational climate to workplace satisfaction (Allen, 2001; Luthans and Youssef, 2007) as well as to institutional effectiveness (Brown and VanWagoner, 1999). An organization's climate can influence an individual's behavior (Baker, 1992), and the climate for managing communications is important in managing conflict (Pettitt and Ayers, 2002).

What and who, then, comprise an organization's climate? Organizational climate refers to the perceptions of the organization's members on the social, political, and physical nature of their personal relationships affecting their ability to work within the organization (Denison, 1996). Constructs such as

WILEY InterScience® DISCOVER SOMETHING GREAT

NEW DIRECTIONS FOR COMMUNITY COLLEGES, no. 142, Summer 2008
Published online in Wiley InterScience (www.interscience.wiley.com) • DOI: 10.1002/cc.324

peer and supervisory support, workplace satisfaction, communication, organizational structure, and collaboration all contribute to a college's organizational climate. Perceived organizational climate influences the attitudes, behavior, and performance of individuals in the organization (Tziner and Dolan, 1984). As to who is involved in organizational climate, the answer is everyone, both males and females, from the student to the maintenance worker to the secretary to the adviser to the faculty member to the president. Everyone involved in the community college shapes the climate of that college, and the climate of the college shapes everyone involved. Understanding the perspectives of all college stakeholders will provide administrators with the necessary knowledge to develop a positive climate for all personnel.

Organizational Climate in Higher Education

While many studies have addressed organizational climate in noneducation organizations, only a few have explored gendered aspects of organizational climate within higher education, and even fewer in a community college setting. Townsend and LaPaglia's study of faculty (2000) in the Chicago community college system, although not a study of climate specifically explored male and female faculty perceptions of administrator attitudes and salary and rank differentials according to gender. They found statistically significant gender-based differences, with women faculty more likely to perceive inequities in salary and rank and less likely to agree that their administrators hold female and male faculty in the same regard. Hagedorn and Laden (2002) found that community college female faculty view college climate in much the same way that their male counterparts do, yet they differ from males in their perceptions of discrimination. Rosser (2004) discovered that gender has an impact on faculty intention to leave when combining faculty work-life perceptions with professional and institutional perceptions. Other research has explored faculty satisfaction, a component of organizational climate. Gibson (2006) examined the impact of the political climate on mentoring of women faculty and found a gender gap in the availability of women in senior faculty positions to serve as mentors as well as concerns about issues of balance for women entering the field.

Research on Noninstructional Staff

Before turning to the scant literature addressing noninstructional staff, we need to better understand some of the terminology involving this specific population. The National Center for Education Statistics (2005) divides higher education staff into two categories: professional staff and nonprofessional staff. Professional staff account for almost 72 percent of all public and private two-year college staff and include those assigned executive, administrative, or managerial positions (4.8 percent), faculty (57 percent), research and instructional assistants (less than 1 percent), and other professionals who provide academic support (9.8 percent). Nonprofessional staff at two-year institutions account for the remaining 28 percent of staff and include technical and paraprofessionals, that is, those with special skills but whose jobs do not require a baccalaureate degree (7.2 percent), clerical and secretarial (14.2 percent), skilled crafts (1 percent), and service and maintenance (11.9 percent). This means that over 45 percent of community college staff do not teach. More than 63 percent are women, and females comprise the majority in all work groups except for service and maintenance. Over 63 percent of nonteaching and nonexecutive professional staff, 61 percent of technical and professional staff, and 85.5 percent of clerical and secretarial staff are women. This contrasts greatly with the 14.4 percent of skilled crafts staff and the 27 percent of service and maintenance staff who are women. Noninstructional staff members are predominantly female. However, only a handful of studies within the past two decades have examined noninstructional staff. Still fewer have included nonprofessional staff, and none have explored noninstructional staff perceptions of college climate from a gendered perspective.

Some of the research on nonteaching staff originated within various community college districts. In 1991, the North Carolina Department of Community Colleges looked at multiple roles among administrative and nonteaching staff, along with colleges' hiring and employee retention experiences during a time of budget restraint. However, this study excluded the gendered aspects of these multiple roles on the employees, on their satisfaction with their job, and any possible effects of multiple job roles on job retention. Nonprofessional staff were also omitted from this study. A few years later, the San Diego Community College District conducted a survey of campus climate among classified staff (Takahata and Armstrong, 1995). This was the first published study on classified staff perceptions of morale and relations, administrative responsiveness, and other aspects of college climate. Although findings were generally positive as to climate, the only separation along gender lines was that men were more likely than women to report they had seen sexist, racist, or homophobic graffiti or had heard disparaging comments about gays and lesbians. It must be noted, however, that 79.2 percent of respondents were female and that respondents were not asked to identify their work group.

More recent research has not originated with the district office. Pettitt and Ayers (2002) assessed organizational climate and conflict communication behaviors of different job groups within a community college following a change in college leadership. Their findings suggest that climate may be related to the use of conflict communication behaviors of individuals. Although this study did assess behavior based on job group, it did not look more closely at the gender breakdown within each group to explore any possible relationship. Van Wagoner (2004) studied the four organizational domains of decision making, programs, support services, and resources by surveying community college professional staff on organizational change. As with previous research, this study omitted nonprofessional staff from its sample and did not examine the influence of gender within the various work groups.

Research Questions

This study explored staff perception of organizational climate, including the impact of gender on staff interactions with faculty and students and staff perceptions of workplace satisfaction within the community college. The overarching research question guiding this study was, What are noninstructional staff perceptions of the community college climate? And there were two related questions: What is the impact of gender on staff interactions with faculty and students? and What is the impact of gender on staff perceptions of workplace satisfaction?

Methodology

This descriptive study used survey research techniques to investigate nonteaching staff perceptions of the community college climate. The survey was anonymous, and respondents did not identify specific community colleges. Sixty items explored work environment: organizational, peer, and supervisory support; task interdependence; faculty-student interactions; job satisfaction; and organizational commitment. Respondents were asked to choose their level of agreement with each statement, using a Likert scale ranging from strongly disagree (1) to strongly agree (5). Questions on organizational, peer, and supervisory support were collapsed into three separate scales, and organizational climate was measured using these scales. Cronbach alphas for these scales were as follows: .80 for the organizational support scale, .86 for the peer support scale, and .80 for the supervisory support scale.

The researcher randomly selected seventy-five public and private two-year institutions in six states within an accrediting region and sent e-mail invitations to all nonteaching staff at those institutions. This resulted in e-mails to 4,020 staff members. Of those e-mails, 162 were returned. Three submissions from faculty members were dropped, resulting in 460 respondents, for a response rate of 12 percent.

Description of Noninstructional Staff

Respondents were placed into work groups using the National Center for Education Statistics definitions (Knapp, Kelly-Reid, Whitmore, and Miller, 2007). Other professionals (46.5 percent) was the largest work group, followed by the clerical and secretarial group (23.9 percent), executives, management, or supervisory staff (22 percent), service and maintenance (6.6 percent), and the skilled crafts group (1.3 percent).

Almost 75 percent of respondents were female, and they were the majority in all work groups except for service and maintenance. Similar numbers of women and men in executive positions reported an annual salary between \$66,000 and \$74,999 (27 percent women, 27.8 percent men), as well as other professionals who reported an annual salary between

$41,000 and $50,999 (31 percent women, 30.4 percent men). Almost 59 percent of female clerical and secretarial staff reported an annual salary between $31,000 and $40,999 as compared to 40 percent of male clerical and secretarial workers. It should be cautioned however, that the data for male clerical workers are skewed due to low numbers in that work group.

The question, "Are you the primary wage earner in your family?" resulted in a significant association with gender. Over 66 percent of females responded that they were the primary wage earner in the family compared with only 33.7 percent of the males. This response is not significant, though, when disaggregated by work groups.

Interactions with Faculty and Students

Six questions addressed issues of faculty and staff interaction, with responses in a Likert format ranging from strongly disagree (1) to strongly agree (5). As detailed in Table 5.1, women's jobs were more likely to require that they interact with faculty and students, but both genders were equally likely to interact with faculty and students even when not required by their jobs. Nonwhite men and women's jobs were more likely to require interaction with faculty and students, and nonwhite women were more likely to interact with faculty and students even when that was not part of their jobs. Overall, respondents were almost equally divided as to having close friends who are faculty members, and they enjoyed helping faculty members and students. Fewer nonwhite women than white women, however, reported having close faculty friends.

Workplace Satisfaction

Seven questions targeted job satisfaction, and eight items looked at organizational commitment, all with responses in a Likert format ranging from strongly disagree (1) to strongly agree (5).

Table 5.1. Faculty and Student Interaction: Percentage of Nonteaching Staff Responding Agree or Strongly Agree by Gender

Item	*Females (n = 342)*	*Males (n = 114)*
My job requires that I interact with faculty and students.	93.5%	84.8%
I interact with students even when it is not part of my job.	85.3	84.8
I have close friends who are faculty members.	50.9	47.8
I enjoy helping faculty members whenever I can.	91.6	86.9
I enjoy helping students whenever I can.	93.7	81.8

Table 5.2. Job Satisfaction: Percentage of Nonteaching Staff Responding Agree or Strongly Agree by Gender

Item	*Females (n = 271)*	*Males (n = 89)*
There is a good fit between what my job offers me and what I look for in a job.	71.0%	68.5%
The job that I currently hold gives me just about everything I want from a job.	52.5	51.7
The demands of this job are a good match to my personal skills.	84.2	83.1
My abilities and training are a good fit with the requirements of this job.	88.9	86.4
My personal abilities and education provide a good match with the demands that my job places on me.	83.6	84.3
My personal values match my institution's values.	65.2	52.8
My institution's values and culture provide a good fit with the things that I value in life.	63.7	56.8

Job Satisfaction. Table 5.2 shows comparative findings of responses to statements dealing with job satisfaction. Overall, respondents were satisfied with their jobs, with levels of satisfaction varying only slightly by gender. Over two-thirds of both men and women viewed their current job as a good fit with what they looked for in a job. They also reported that the demands of their current job were a good match to their personal skills, abilities and training, and education. Women were more likely than men to respond that their institution's values and culture provided a good fit with their values. Women who had been at their current job for ten or more years, were primary wage earners, and worked between eleven and twenty hours per week also reported higher overall levels of job satisfaction.

Examining job satisfaction by work group and gender provides additional insight. Overall, female executive staff reported higher levels of satisfaction with their job when compared to any other work group. Female service and maintenance staff were the least satisfied of all work groups, with male service and maintenance staff overall being more satisfied than their female counterparts. While over two-thirds of both female and male executives viewed their current job as a good fit with what they looked for in a job, less than two-thirds of male and less than one-third of female service and maintenance staff were as satisfied with job fit. Female service and maintenance staff were least likely to agree or strongly agree that the demands of their job were a good match to their personal skills and their education. Women executives and service staff were more likely to respond that their institution's values and culture provided a good fit with what they value in life as opposed to the males in their work groups.

Organizational Commitment. Responses to questions on organizational commitment differed slightly by gender, with women appearing to be overall more committed to their institutions than men were. Gender differences in responses were significant in two instances. Women were more likely to report feeling as though they belonged at their community college ($t(350) = 2.03$, $p = .043$) and that they enjoyed working for their institution ($t(350) = 2.11$, $p = .035$). Otherwise respondents agreed or strongly agreed that they were proud to tell others that they worked at their institution, would be happy to work for their institution until they retire, were satisfied with their jobs, and felt as though their institutions deserved their loyalty (women's responses were slightly higher than those of the men). Responses also varied by work groups. Female executive staff and clerical staff were more likely to agree or strongly agree with all organizational commitment statements than were respondents in other work groups.

Perceptions of Organizational Climate. Organizational climate was measured by a peer support scale, an organizational support scale, and a supervisory support scale. Overall, responses differed by gender on all three scales, with response means higher from women than the men (see Table 5.3). Peer group support, however, was the only scale that differed significantly ($t(339) = 3.07$, $p = .002$) across gender. Viewing perceptions of organizational climate through the work groups shows some definite shifts. Although perceptions of supervisory support differed significantly ($F(4,338) = 2.405$, $p = .049$) by work group, with service and maintenance staff responses

Table 5.3. Perceptions of Organizational Climate by Gender

Item	*Females* (*n* = 271) *M (SD)*	*Males* (*n* = 89) *M (SD)*
Peer Support Scale	3.80(.58)*	3.54(.829)*
Executive, administrative, managerial staff	3.86(.09)	3.52(.13)
Other professional staff	3.76(.57)	3.78(.61)
Clerical and secretarial staff	3.83(.55)	3.51(.97)
Service and maintenance staff	3.77(.64)	3.32(1.01)
Supervisory Support Scale	3.51(.65)	3.42(.79)
Executive, administrative, managerial staff	3.60(.66)	3.53(.58)
Other professional staff	3.44(.66)	3.64(.64)
Clerical and secretarial staff	3.58(.58)	3.22(1.23)
Service and maintenance staff	3.55(.58)	3.05(1.05)
Organizational Support Scale	3.58(.68)	3.45(.72)
Executive, administrative, managerial staff	3.72(.61)	3.31(.68)
Other professional staff	3.47(.70)	3.60(.62)
Clerical and secretarial staff	3.73(.64)	3.33(1.50)
Service and maintenance staff	3.62(.44)	3.32(.81)

*$p < .05$.

significantly lower than those offered by the executive work group, gender differences within the work groups were not significant. Female executive staff provided the highest ratings overall, giving peer support the highest ratings, followed by organizational support, and then supervisory support. Male service and maintenance staff provided the lowest ratings overall, giving organizational and peer support the highest ratings and supervisory support the lowest.

Discussion

This study explored gendered perceptions of community college noninstructional staff to determine the impact of gender on their interactions with students and faculty, their perceptions of campus climate, and their perceptions of workplace satisfaction. Despite being a descriptive study, the findings afford much insight into the college climate through the eyes of noninstructional staff.

Townsend (2006) delved into the issues of what constitutes a positive organizational climate for women and minorities in the community college, suggesting that we need to be cognizant of how our cultural assumptions, spoken or not, affect the ability and willingness to change the college climate. Applying this suggestion to the current study, do we assume that female staff will be more nurturing of students and faculty than male staff will be? Do we assume that noninstructional staff are all alike, with all holding the same views, values, and goals? Studies such as the current one will help us recognize the sometimes gendered lens through which we may be viewing noninstructional staff.

This study suggests several strategies and research topics worthy of consideration. First, there is a need for continued dialogue and education concerning college climate and gender. Everyone responsible for crafting the community college workplace should be educated as to the gendered perspectives of nonteaching staff job satisfaction as well as the influence of college climate on job satisfaction. Once leaders and others understand the components of climate and the gendered nature of any underlying practices and perceptions affecting the climate, steps can be taken to change the climate to meet the needs of all employees.

Leaders also need a better understanding of the impact of gender on staff interaction, particularly interaction with students. Interaction with coworkers has been connected to employee and customer retention (Alexandrov, Babakus, and Yavas, 2007); a case can be made that staff interaction with students also is important to their retention as community college "customers." Interaction has been linked to organizational climate as contributing to workplace satisfaction (Schuetz, 2005), and studying the gendered relationships that occur between staff and faculty and staff and students will help leaders to better understand college climate. Leaders who understand college climate are better able to effect change.

Regular assessment of employee job satisfaction, coupled with employee perceptions of and satisfaction with college climate, is vital for leaders who want to craft a climate that supports all employees. Although researchers tend to assess employee satisfaction, colleges seldom grasp the opportunity to do so. Colleges that want to reduce employee turnover, improve morale, and strengthen organizational commitment need to understand their employees' satisfaction with their jobs, as well as colleges' climate to help guide action in maintaining satisfaction.

More knowledge on the link between work group gender composition and job satisfaction is also necessary. Leaders who understand the impact of gender-balanced work groups on such issues as job satisfaction, turnover intent, organizational commitment, and organizational climate can better press for change or design effective solutions for problem areas. While research has explored the connection between employee satisfaction and work group gender diversity across business organizations (Fields and Blum, 1997), this topic has not been studied in the community college setting. Leaders aware of such issues can then direct the necessary resources (for example, incentives for the individual or access to an internal candidate pool for hiring and promotion) inward toward personalized career development programs and support and outward toward recruitment. Helping both women and men acquire the skills and training in areas where they are normally underrepresented to increase their numbers in those areas is likely to improve employee perceptions and satisfaction, leading to lower turnover.

Since work environment is an important component of job and climate satisfaction, a final strategy is to strengthen the support systems within the college. The supervisor, for instance, is important to college climate in a variety of ways. A supervisor's communication or human resource skills are vital in creating a positive climate for career development through skill development support, performance appraisal, and fostering peer support. In many instances, supervisors serve in a gatekeeping capacity by disseminating information about the college and the climate. Supervisors who lack the necessary communication skills or communicate with some gender bias could well harm an employee's satisfaction with job and climate. Although the quality of supervision was not part of this study, the gendered aspects of supervision need to be addressed, particularly in non-gender-balanced work groups. Providing training and education on workplace satisfaction, the gendered aspects of communication, and how to foster a climate of support are necessary when striving to improve the climate for all. Further research into the impact of supervisors on college climate and job satisfaction will also prove helpful.

References

Allen, T. "Family-Supportive Work Environments: The Role of Organizational Perceptions." *Journal of Vocational Behavior,* 2001, *58,* 414–435.

Alexandrov, A., Babakus, E., and Yavas, U. "The Effects of Perceived Management Concern for Front-Line Employees and Customers on Turnover Intentions." *Journal of Service Research,* 2007, *9*(4), 356–371.

Baker, G. A. *Cultural Leadership: Inside America's Community Colleges.* Washington, D.C.: Community College Press, 1992.

Brown, J. D., and VanWagoner, R. J. "Organizational Climate: The Overlooked Dimension of Institutional Effectiveness." Paper presented at the Thirty-Ninth Annual Forum of the Association for Institutional Research, Seattle, Wash., May 1999.

Denison, D. R. "What Is the Difference Between Organizational Culture and Organizational Climate? A Native's Point of View on a Decade of Paradigm Wars." *Academy of Management Review,* 1996, *21*(3), 619–654.

Fields, D. L., and Blum, T. C. "Employee Satisfaction in Work Groups with Different Gender Composition." *Journal of Organizational Behavior,* 1997, *18,* 181–186.

Gibson, S. K. "Mentoring of Women Faculty: The Role of Organizational Politics and Climate." *Innovative Higher Education,* 2006, *31*(1), 63–79.

Hagedorn, L. S., and Laden, B. V. "Exploring the Climate for Women as Community College Faculty." In C. L. Outcalt (ed.), *Community College Faculty: Characteristics, Practices, and Challenges.* New Directions for Community Colleges, no. 118. San Francisco: Jossey-Bass, 2002.

Knapp, L. G., Kelly-Reid, J. E., Whitmore, R. W., and Miller, E. *Employees in Postsecondary Institutions, Fall 2005, and Salaries of Full-Time Instructional Faculty, 2005–06.* Washington, D.C.: National Center for Education Statistics, 2007.

Luthans, F., and Youssef, C. M. "Emerging Positive Organizational Behavior." *Journal of Management,* 2007, *33*(3), 321–349.

National Center for Education Statistics. *Employees in Degree-Granting Institutions, by Employment Status, Sex, Control and Type of Institution, and Primary Occupation: Fall 2003.* Washington, D.C.: National Center for Education Statistics, 2005.

North Carolina Department of Community Colleges. *Administrator and Non-Teaching Professionals Survey: 1990–1991.* Raleigh: North Carolina Department of Community Colleges, 1991.

Pettitt, J. M., and Ayers, D. F. "Understanding Conflict and Climate in a Community College." *Community College Journal of Research and Practice,* 2002, *26,* 105–120.

Rosser, V. J. "Faculty Members' Intentions to Leave: A National Study on Their Worklife and Satisfaction." *Research in Higher Education,* 2004, *45*(3), 285–309.

Schuetz, P. "UCLA Community College Review: Campus Environment: A Missing Link in Studies of Community College Retention." *Community College Review,* 2005, *32*(4), 60–80.

Takahata, G. M., and Armstrong, D. B. *Campus Climate Classified Staff Survey.* San Diego, Calif.: San Diego Community College District, 1995.

Townsend, B. K. "Community College Organizational Climate for Minorities and Women." *Community College Journal of Research and Practice,* 2006, *30,* 813–826.

Townsend, B. K., and LaPaglia, N. "The Community College as a Workplace for Women Faculty Members." *Initiatives,* 2000, *59*(4), n.p.

Tziner, A., and Dolan, S. "The Relationship of Two Sociodemographic Variables and Perceived Climate Dimensions to Performance." *Canadian Journal of Administrative Sciences,* 1984, *1,* 272–287.

Van Wagoner, R. J. "Influencing the Perception of Organizational Change in Community Colleges." *Community College Journal of Research and Practice,* 2004, *28,* 715–727.

MOLLY H. DUGGAN is assistant professor of community college leadership in the department of educational leadership and counseling at Old Dominion University.

6

This chapter presents findings from a study of faculty governance in community colleges, focusing on involvement, perceptions, and experiences of faculty with an emphasis on the differences between men and women faculty.

The Actors Behind the Curtain: Representation of Women Faculty in Community College Institutional Decision Making

Jaime Lester, Scott Lukas

One of the major hallmarks of postsecondary education is shared governance. As an organizational structure that promotes collegial government, shared governance is an integral part of decision making within postsecondary institutions; it affords faculty a voice in academic decisions, such as curriculum, hiring and promotion, admissions, and student retention (American Association of University Professors, 1966). The involvement of faculty promotes inclusiveness and democracy within colleges and universities. Community colleges that have a strong tradition in democracy and civic responsibility have traditionally had strong faculty governance bodies. National studies indicate that approximately 70 percent of all community colleges have such a faculty governance body (Gilmour, 1991). Although these bodies have a variety of titles—such as faculty senate, academic senate, and faculty association—the purpose is generally to provide faculty voice in institutional decision making (Garavalia, Miller, and Miles, 1999).

Shared governance has been a common structure within community colleges, but the participation and involvement of faculty has varied dramatically. Women faculty are underrepresented in faculty governance leadership positions despite the fact that women faculty traditionally conduct more service work (Eveline, 2004; Pope and Miller, 2000; Tierney and

NEW DIRECTIONS FOR COMMUNITY COLLEGES, no. 142, Summer 2008 © 2008 Wiley Periodicals, Inc.
Published online in Wiley InterScience (www.interscience.wiley.com) • DOI: 10.1002/cc.325

Bensimon, 1996). Armstrong (1999) found that the level of participation of women is quite high but that women generally do not hold leadership positions; rather, they serve on committees that address admissions, curriculum, and faculty searches, while men participate on tenure, strategic planning, and policy committees (Twale and Shannon, 1996). The committees in which men more frequently participate are often those that hold more power within the institution, and these committees make decisions with the greatest impact. In order to more fully understand why gender disparities emerge within faculty governance, it is important to examine the perceptions of involvement and the experiences of male and female faculty. The inequitable involvement of faculty threatens the democratic values of community colleges and calls into question the purpose of faculty governance to represent all faculty issues. Furthermore, engaging and empowering diverse groups of faculty will better situate community colleges to successfully grapple with external and internal forces that place increased stress on community colleges: increased accountability, competition from proprietary colleges, large-scale retirements of both administrators and faculty, and an increase in the level of part-time faculty.

The purpose of this study is to further the examination of involvement, perceptions, and experiences of faculty in shared governance, with an emphasis on the differences between men and women. Moreover, this study seeks to understand potential gender disparities in the experience of women faculty while involved in shared governance, with a focus on harassment, discrimination, and involvement. The study is guided by the following research questions:

- Do gender differences exist in the level of involvement in faculty governance?
- Do the perceptions of the governance process, the power of faculty governance, and the role of faculty in campus governance vary by gender?
- Do male and female community college faculty experience differing levels of discrimination during involvement in faculty governance?

Following is a discussion and description of faculty governance structures within community colleges, with an emphasis on California, the site for this study, and a discussion of the research on gender differences in involvement, satisfaction, and perceptions of faculty governance. We end with the results and recommendations for practice.

Faculty Governance in Community College

Shared governance is a common structure within institutional decision making in community colleges. With approximately three-fourths of all community colleges having shared governance bodies (Gilmour, 1991), faculty generally have a strong influence in decisions regarding curriculum, policies, and student life. However, shared governance in a community college setting is not uniform (Birnbaum, 1988; Gilmour, 1991); there are a variety of definitions and types of shared governing units. While some community colleges have faculty senates, others have faculty associations or college councils. In some cases, overlapping bureaucracies of local, district, and statewide levels bear on the effectiveness of shared governance, as does competition among shared governance groups, such as the academic senate and faculty union. The way in which the individual community college and the community college district is structured in terms of the faculty senate also has a profound impact on the influence of the faculty. Statewide governance structures include a number of categories—from federal states (Illinois, Washington) that have separate, statewide coordinating structures for community colleges and local governing boards, to unified states (Alaska, Hawaii, Idaho, Montana, Nevada, North and South Dakota, Rhode Island, and Utah) that feature a single board that governs all degree-granting institutions (Richardson and de los Santos, 2001).

Not only are shared governance units within community colleges variable, the types of issues addressed are also quite diverse (Kater and Levin, 2004). Armstrong (1999) found in a study of an urban community college in Alabama that the faculty senate discussed a diverse set of issues ranging from budgets to smoking policies. Miller (2003) noted that senates cover issues related to faculty life, workload, evaluation, contracts, facilities, and planning. The most frequent issues discussed are faculty workload and budgetary items, such as salary and benefits. Other variation across institutions includes the way in which leadership is established within the governance structure. In California, the use of overworked faculty contributes to a condition in which it is difficult to find officers or representatives to serve in academic senates. While the majority of governance units use elected leadership teams to manage their work, others rely on individual elections or administrative appointive leaders (Miller, 2003).

The ideal of the shared governance model is collegial, provides rewards, assists in maximizing system efficiency, and assists in the sharing of resources (Lau, 1998; Howell, 1997). However in community colleges, the ideals of shared governance have not necessarily been achieved. While a large majority of community colleges report having shared governance, not all of the colleges have substantial involvement. Within multicollege districts in California, there is the issue of equal involvement of all colleges in the district governance structure, while small districts (including single-college ones) may perceive that they are not included in statewide decision making, as large or multicollege districts are. Furthermore, having a shared governance structure does not necessarily mean that all individuals have equal power within the process. When individual groups are disenfranchised or marginalized within the governance structure, their level of participation is not indicative of their actual influence within institutional decision-making processes. Without equal participation, shared governance becomes nothing more than an ineffective governing unit that ceases to represent the faculty.

Traditionally in large public universities, the proportion of women participating in campus governance has remained low (Baldridge, Curtis, Ecker, and Riley, 1978; Taylor and Shavlik, 1977). One of the reasons for the low-level involvement was the lack of women in faculty roles and the lack of women in tenured positions. Yet recent data indicate that the involvement of women in faculty governance has not increased dramatically despite larger numbers of women in faculty tenure roles (Twale and Shannon, 1996). When women are part of faculty governance, their perception of power and influence is lower than that of their male colleagues. Women often feel that they have less power within the campus hierarchy and a lower level of understanding of how the power and authority structure operates (Twale and Shannon, 1996). What is less known are the reasons that women continue to be disproportionately underrepresented in faculty governance units and the level at which women faculty feel empowered and influential while involved in the governance process. This study seeks to understand the level at which women faculty are involved in faculty governance and whether they experience harassment and discrimination within the context of governance.

Method

In order to examine the impact of gender on campus participation and satisfaction with governance, the authors conducted a survey of faculty in one large statewide community college system.

Instrumentation. The survey instrument used in the study was drawn from a thorough review of the literature and a survey conducted by Twale and Shannon (1996) on gender differences among faculty and campus governance. The four-part survey assessed faculty involvement in campus governance, perceptions of governance, perceptions of power in campus governance, role of faculty in campus governance, and perceptions of the impact of gender in involvement and participation in campus governance. Questions of involvement in campus governments were used to assess the number of committees, frequency of participation, and whether the individual faculty held leadership roles within governance committees. Satisfaction with each of these areas was measured on a four-point Likert scale. Perceptions of governance power and involvement were measured on a five-point Likert scale with questions addressing communication, rewards, and the representation of faculty in the decision-making process. The final section on the survey measures the extent to which men and women faculty experienced discrimination and hostility while involved in campus governance. Questions related to harassment, ability to be effectively involved, retaliation, and exclusion were included in the survey. In addition, demographic questions were added to compare across gender, status, and years of experience. Open-ended questions were included to elicit additional information on participation and satisfaction with governance.

Participants. The sample for this study consisted of individuals within the California community colleges. We chose these colleges because California has a formalized governance process (including a statewide academic senate) that traditionally has a strong influence on each campus and within the faculty union. The survey was sent to each of the presidents of the individual academic senates in the 109 California community colleges, who were asked to disseminate the electronic link to the survey to their campus faculty. The resulting sample was 696. Demographically the sample represents current trends in faculty populations, with a majority of the sample being women (60 percent), Caucasian (73 percent), full-time tenured (69 percent), in the social sciences or humanities (50 percent), and with an average time of thirteen years at the institution. The sample did not differ on any of the demographic variables except for discipline. Men were more likely than women to be in the sciences.

Data Analysis. To understand potential differences in gender and involvement, satisfaction, perceptions of power, and the impact of gender on involvement and participation, we conducted both descriptive and inferential statistics. Factor analysis was conducted using internal consistency estimates to create scales for perceptions of power and discrimination. The data were initially analyzed for frequency distributions with follow-up means tests, including *t*-tests and analysis of variance.

Results

Results from this study indicate that women community college faculty generally feel as if they are fairly represented and satisfied in campus governance. The following outlines the results by highlighting perceptions and satisfaction with involvement, perceptions of power, and discrimination.

Involvement. In order to understand the level of involvement of male and female faculty in campus governance, we conducted frequencies on the degree of involvement in campus governance, whether faculty served in a leadership role, the types of committees they served on, satisfaction with involvement, and the availability of rewards for participation in governance. The majority of male faculty (65 percent) indicated that they were either highly or moderately involved in campus governance; female faculty reported similar rates (62 percent). Results indicated that male and female faculty participate in campus governance at similar rates and that they had similar levels of satisfaction. Approximately 75 percent of male faculty and 76 percent of female faculty were either very satisfied or moderately satisfied with their involvement in campus governance. Subsequent analysis of variance tests showed no significant differences between male and female faculty.

Additional analyses were also conducted to test for significant differences based on tenure status, discipline, and gender. Although no statistical significance was found between or among these groups, several of the participants noted the importance of having tenure before becoming involved in governance. One faculty member noted, "Be tenured first so you cannot become a target of overzealous administrators wishing to retaliate for your participation in faculty governance." Another faculty member noted, "Have tenure before pursuing any designated leadership role such as a senator or a committee chair. Use tenure-track time to observe, learn, and serve."

Although both male and female faculty were highly involved in campus governance, we also wanted to understand if they served in leadership roles at the same rates. Both male and female faculty reported similar rates of involvement as leaders or officers within campus governance. Approximately 38 percent of male and female faculty had been in a leadership role in campus governance, and approximately 34 percent of males and females have served as an officer. The majority of faculty have served on one or more committees, with female faculty having a slightly higher, yet not statistically significant, rate of participation on social and curricular committees and male faculty having higher representation on planning committees.

The only area of involvement that showed a more substantial difference between male and female faculty was related to their perceptions of rewards. Although the difference between groups is not statistically significant, women faculty were less likely to report that institutions provided rewards, such as reassigned time or monetary subsidies, and were also less likely to report that faculty currently receive rewards for participation in campus governance. In California, matters like reassigned time are often negotiated with the union and administration and are thus highly variable. Several women faculty agreed with this statement: "The only way to know the issues and to influence outcome is to become involved. Our college faculty and administrators respect involved faculty. The drawback is the additional time required, with little compensation until one is elected to a major office like academic senate president, for meaningful effort." Since the level of involvement between male and female faculty was very similar, the difference noted in rewards suggests that rewards given for campus involvement are unequal between the genders.

Perceptions of Power. Faculty were asked to evaluate the level and frequency of communication among faculty governance units, the board of trustees, and academic administrators. Results indicated that both male and female faculty agreed that faculty governance was effectively communicating with the board of trustees and academic administrators. The mean of the communication scale was approximately 3.6 for males and 3.7 for female faculty. Although male and female faculty had similar perceptions of communication among faculty governance units, the board, and academic administrators, the mean indicates only a moderate feeling regarding the overall communication: a mean of 3.5 falls between neutral and agree on the Likert scale. This finding suggests that both male and female faculty felt that the communication between faculty governance, boards, and academic administrators was somewhat low.

The next scale that addressed perceptions of power of the faculty governance was the support scale, which measured the extent to which faculty feel as if they are empowered to question policy decisions and whether they agree that information was available to the faculty governance body to address campuswide issues. Similar to the communication scale, both male and female faculty expressed similar views of the level of support that faculty governance receives, with a mean of approximately 3.3 representing only a moderate view of support. Again, differences between genders did not emerge as significant, and both groups felt that governance received a moderate level of support. No significant differences were found on any of the single-item measures or the communication and support scale.

The final measure of perception of power includes several single-item measures: the level at which faculty governance is involved in decision making, the representation of faculty governance on committees that make decisions on policies, the level at which faculty must insist on rights and responsibilities within the institution, and faculty involvement in developing specific outcomes for budgetary expenditures. Over half of male and female faculty reported that they felt that faculty governance was involved in decision making, and two-thirds of male and female faculty noted that faculty were represented on committees that make policy decisions. Despite these findings, several faculty described their frustration with the lack of power of faculty governance. One male faculty member explained, "Don't bother . . . . it's all form and no substance. We are never empowered to decide; only to recommend . . . in the end, the administration always does as it wishes." Another male faculty member took a longer perspective of the power of faculty governance: "As faculty we do have the power to change the institution for the betterment of our students. The negative is that decisions are very slow. It may take several months."

Statistically significant differences were found between male and female full-time tenured faculty. Women faculty were more likely to feel as if there needed to be greater representation in faculty governance on committees that made decisions on policies. Results also indicated that although faculty felt that they were represented on committees and participate in important decisions, faculty governance must insist on rights and responsibilities and faculty should be more involved in budgetary expenditures. Women full-time tenured faculty were more likely to feel that faculty should be more involved in developing outcomes for budgets.

One female faculty member explained, "At this point it seems like a waste of time as faculty have zero power to effect administrative policies and spending." Therefore, faculty note that they are currently involved in decisions, but feel as if their involvement needs to be increased, and women faculty who are full time and tenured are more likely to feel that there needs to be more faculty involvement in budgets and more faculty representation on decision-making committees.

One of the reasons that a difference emerged among full-time tenured faculty is due to the lack of involvement of part-time and nontenured faculty. Because the sample size of this study does not reflect a large enough representation of part-time faculty, it is difficult to draw conclusions about the feelings and perceptions of part-time faculty. Yet one faculty member noted, "This is irrelevant to part-time faculty in my system. Our voices are not heard, not solicited. The union works to keep all power in the hands of the full timers, though the part timers make up 40 percent of the faculty. My best advice is to decertify the union and create one that uses parity for part timers as its basis—and that includes governance."

Discrimination. The final area of analysis concerns feelings of discrimination during involvement in faculty governance. The feelings of discrimination scale measured the extent to which faculty felt excluded, retaliated against, harassed during participation, and harassed while voicing opinions. Overall the faculty indicated that they did not feel that they were discriminated against while involved in faculty governance (mean = 2.23). Next, we examined gender differences on the feelings of discrimination scale. Interestingly, women were slightly less likely to feel as if they experienced discrimination. The mean for men on the discrimination scale was 2.30, and for women it was 2.18. In the open-ended questions, several women noted that they thought they were well represented in faculty governance committees and the women appeared to be "taking over" faculty governance. One woman noted, "I think women are well represented in faculty governance committees." However, some women participants noted that women still experience discrimination: "If you are an intelligent, competent woman, you are definitely a threat to the old boys' club. Our campus is quite misogynist."

No significant differences were found between male and female faculty and the discrimination scale, but they were found between disciplines and discrimination. Social sciences and humanities and vocational and technical education disciplines differed in their responses to feelings of discrimination. Women in the social sciences experienced more discrimination. One of the male faculty participants provided some insight into the reasons for differences by discipline: "I do not view myself as sexist; however since my entire administration has become female, my department, which is voc ed, has suffered tremendously." This comment speaks to the potential gender discrimination that occurs within the disciplines and the backlash of women entering traditionally male fields.

The second scale is the influence during participation scale, which measures the extent to which faculty feel that their participation is taken seriously and that they are listened to by their colleagues. The majority of the faculty feel that their colleagues both listen to them and take their comments seriously (mean = 4.0). The mean for men and women faculty on the influence during participation scale was almost identical, at 3.97. This indicates that male and female faculty have no statistical differences in terms of their feelings of influence in faculty governance. Also, no differences emerged by discipline, status, or gender on the influence during participation scale.

In the open-ended questions, the majority of individuals indicated that gender does not appear to be an issue in campus governance and used the representation of women as evidence for equity and governance. A small minority of participants, however, expressed concern regarding the equal participation and influence of women in campus governance. One woman noted, "The words of men are taken more seriously and are heard more loudly, although women on our campus hold more leadership positions and produce more of the documentation leading to outcomes." Another woman stated, "While there are plenty of committee chairs who are women, the men in the room always seem to have the greatest influence. They are more forceful in their opinions and better at directing the flow of the discourse."

Conclusion and Implications

Campus governance is a system that exists on the majority of community college campuses across the nation. Although community colleges vary by mission and influence, the democratic values and philosophy that serve as a foundation for shared governance provide an ethos of equity. Faculty come together as nonsexist, nonracist, and nongendered individuals to participate in institutional processes and practices. In reality, they do experience discrimination during their involvement and participation in faculty governance, but they are often less likely to feel that their participation is laden with discriminatory beliefs and values. Many of the responses on the open-ended questions speak to this hidden form of discrimination that pervades shared governance. For example, women are less likely to participate in influential planning (budget and tenure and promotion committees), and representation in shared governance does not extend to all faculty. One faculty member noted, "Part timers are the majority of faculty on all our CA campuses, yet they are viewed as invisible when it comes to decision-making and governance. This should be changed ASAP. I believe in equal pay for equal work, respect and at least shared offices for part-time faculty. Our unions, senates, are not democratic with equal access, equal representation, and they certainly should be." Although there are issues within campus governance, there are steps that community colleges can take in order to address the subversive discrimination.

Evaluation. We suggest that faculty governance leaders in campus administrations systematically evaluate levels of involvement within both the overall faculty governance and specific committees, with attention to diversity in terms of gender, race, discipline, and sexuality. Regular surveys of faculty can help determine the level of participation of faculty and faculty satisfaction with their participation in collegial governance. Additional analysis should include interviews and observations of faculty governance activities in order to examine the level at which men and women are involved and able to influence governance activities. As well, faculty should survey not only the extent of their involvement in campus governance but its effect. Faculty may be theoretically involved in shared governance, but their recommendations may be ignored or minimized. It is thus important to assess the result of faculty involvement in governance.

Recruitment. Faculty and administrators should consider mentoring programs, strategic recruitment efforts, and term limits in order to increase the diversity of individuals on influential committees. For example, a budget committee member could have a two- to three-year term limit with an expectation of having a diverse committee composition. Committee members should be expected to mentor new faculty to take over committee responsibilities when term limits expire.

Inclusiveness. College governance needs to consider the importance of part-time faculty in institutional decision making. Not only are full-time faculty becoming overwhelmed within shared governance, part-time faculty who actively participate in teaching and learning within the institution are often disenfranchised (Kezar, Lester, and Anderson, 2006). As the numbers of part-time faculty continue to increase, the involvement of part-time faculty is crucial to maintaining campus governance and promoting equity within governance.

Alternative Models. Effective shared governance should include the participation of all groups, including students, administrators, classified staff, and trustees. In some areas, however, there may not be agreement between faculty representing different groups, such as the academic senate, the collective bargaining unit, or union (Academic Senate of California Community Colleges, 1996). Assessing alternative models for effective participation between faculty governance bodies that may have different mandates should be explored. California, for example, maintains active faculty unions as well as individual faculty senates on each campus. Faculty senate and union representatives work together and are equally represented on respective boards.

Workload. As indicated by the survey, faculty often perceive workload to be a block in effectively participating in campus governance. Community college faculty are often overworked, and sometimes their involvement in campus governance committees is uncompensated. As a result, they may choose to withdraw from campus decision making. Individual campuses should look at the workload distribution and assess whether excessive workload or uncompensated work in governance has negative effects on faculty involvement in shared governance.

Communication. One of the most significant ways in which faculty can remain involved in governance is through effective communication. Many community college academic senates and unions have official newsletters or Web sites that discuss governance matters. Whereas administrators and boards of trustees meet regularly to discuss governance, faculty are sometimes atomized—in part due to differences among disciplines, different work schedules, or lack of attendance at important campus meetings. Faculty should work on effective models of communication and use these to share information among their constituents; as well, an effort should be made to involve part-time faculty in this communication.

References

Academic Senate of California Community Colleges. *Developing a Model for Effective Senate and Union Relations.* Sacramento: Academic Senate of California Community Colleges, 1996.

American Association of University Professors. *Statement on the Governance of College and Universities.* Washington, D.C.: American Association of University Professors, 1966.

Armstrong, W. P. "Trends and Issues of a Community College Faculty Senate: Jefferson State Community College, 1987–1997." Unpublished doctoral dissertation, University of Alabama, Tuscaloosa, 1999.

Baldridge, J., Curtis, D., Ecker, G., and Riley, G. *Policy-Making and Effective Leadership.* San Francisco: Jossey-Bass, 1978.

Birnbaum, R. *How Colleges Work.* San Francisco: Jossey-Bass, 1988.

Eveline, J. *Ivory Basement Leadership: Power and Invisibility in the Changing University.* Perth: University of Western Australia Press, 2004.

Garavalia, B., Miller, M., and Miles, A. "Trends and Issues of a Community College: Jefferson State Community College, 1987–1997." Paper presented at the Council for the Study of Community Colleges Conference, Nashville, Tenn., Apr. 1999.

Gilmour, J. "Participative Governance Bodies in Higher Education: Report of a National Study." In R. Birnbaum (ed.), *Faculty in Governance: The Role of Senates and Joint Committees in Academic Decision-Making.* New Directions for Higher Education, no. 75. San Francisco: Jossey-Bass, 1991.

Howell, C. D. "An Assessment of the Implementation of Shared Governance Provisions of AB 1725 at Selected California Community Colleges." *Community College Journal of Research and Practice,* 1997, *21*(7), 637–649.

Kater, S., and Levin, J. S. "Shared Governance in the Community College." *Community College Journal of Research and Practice,* 2004, *29*(2), 1–23.

Kezar, A., Lester, J., and Anderson, G. "Lacking Courage, Corporate Sellout, Not a Real Faculty Member: Challenging Stereotypes That Prevent Effective Governance." *NEA: Thought and Action,* 2006, *221,* 121–134.

Lau, R. "Shared Governance Under Siege: Is It Time to Revive It or Get Rid of It?" *Chronicle of Higher Education,* Jan. 30, 1998, pp. A8–A9.

Miller, M. T. "The Status of Faculty Senates in Community Colleges." *Community College Journal of Research and Practice,* 2003, 27(5), 419–428.

Pope, M. L., and Miller M. T. "Community College Faculty Governance Leaders: Results of a National Survey." *Community College Journal of Research and Practice,* 2000, *24,* 627–638.

Richardson, R., and de los Santos, G. "Statewide Governance Structures and Two-Year Colleges." In B. Townsend and S. B. Twombly (eds.), *Community Colleges: Policy in the Future Context.* Stamford, Conn.: Ablex, 2001.

Taylor, E., and Shavlik, D. "To Advance Women: A National Identification Program." *Educational Record,* 1977, *58*(1), 91–100.
Tierney, W. G., and Bensimon, E. M. *Promotion and Tenure: Community and Socialization in Academe.* Albany: State University of New York Press, 1996.
Twale, D. J., and Shannon, D. M. "Gender Differences Among Faculty in Campus Governance: Nature of Involvement, Satisfaction, and Power." *Initiatives,* 1996, *57*(4), 11–19.

JAIME LESTER is assistant professor of higher education at George Mason University.

SCOTT LUKAS is instructor and department chair for the sociology department at Lake Tahoe Community College.

7

This chapter provides a portrait of women's representation in the leadership ranks of community colleges and reviews data on how six women presidents talk about their lived experiences at the helm of their institutions. Findings indicate an uneven playing field for women on their way to a presidency.

Gendered Leadership: An Organizational Perspective

Pamela L. Eddy, Elizabeth M. Cox

Community colleges are regarded as democratic institutions, admitting anyone through open access and bringing educational opportunity to those not welcomed at many other institutions. Among the individuals welcomed at community colleges are those considered of low socioeconomic status, the unemployed, minority group members, and new immigrants to the United States. Yet those who occupy the leadership roles of the "people's colleges" do not mirror the diversity that is represented in community college enrollments. Women fill only 29 percent of all community college presidencies (American Council on Education, 2007), whereas they comprise 57 percent of students at these institutions (National Center for Education Statistics, 2004). Thus, the bulk of current community college leaders are members of the dominant class, race, and sex.

The next decade is predicted to see dramatic changes within community college leadership in the United States. According to the American Association of Community Colleges, almost 80 percent of current community college presidents plan to retire by 2011 (Shults, 2001). Indeed, the American Council on Education's recent survey of community college presidents shows that 44 percent are over sixty-one years of age (American Council on Education, 2007). This dramatic statistic places a strain on the community college system and puts leadership development in the forefront of issues facing community colleges. Will this mass exodus of presidential leadership, currently dominated by middle-aged white males, open the door for women and minorities to have more of a presence in community college

WILEY InterScience® DISCOVER SOMETHING GREAT

NEW DIRECTIONS FOR COMMUNITY COLLEGES, no. 142, Summer 2008 © 2008 Wiley Periodicals, Inc.
Published online in Wiley InterScience (www.interscience.wiley.com) • DOI: 10.1002/cc.326

leadership, or is the organizational culture of community colleges such that the status quo will be replicated and maintained? Currently less than one-third of two-year presidents are women, and this representation has not changed significantly in the past five years (American Council on Education, 2007). This chapter describes research conducted to create a portrait of women leading community colleges and examines the influence of gendered organizational structures.

Leadership Overview

Amey and Twombly (1992) studied leadership at community colleges and concluded that the language used to recount the organizational development of the community college sector reinforced male norms for leadership; it was based on research by and about a relatively small collection of white male scholars and practitioners. Research on women's leadership clearly documents that women are judged against male norms (Chliwniak, 1997; Monroehurst, 1997). Kanter (1993) noted the masculine ethic in management and the feminization of clerical work and concluded that bureaucratic structures give power through activities and alliances, most often to the exclusion of women. Little has changed in organizational structures since Kanter posited this relationship over a decade ago. Acker (1990) coined the concept of gendered organizations to highlight the advantages the male norm brings to the distribution of power. Organizations are the "products and producers of gender-based power relations, and . . . masculine ways of doing things are inherent in structural, ideological and symbolic aspects of organization, as well as in everyday interactions and practices" (Hatch and Cunliffe, 2006, p. 274). Acker's framework served as the backdrop for this study.

Acker (1990) argued that gender is not an addition to ongoing processes but is instead an integral part of those processes. Acker posited that gendering in organizations occurs in at least five interacting processes: the construction of divisions along gender lines; the construction of symbols and images that explain, reinforce, or oppose those divisions; the interactions between women and men, women and women, and men and men that enact dominance and submission; the production of gendered components of individual identity; and the ongoing processes of creating and conceptualizing social structures. An example of this gendering is the conceptualization of the job and job evaluation. Within organizations, jobs are seen as being separate from individuals; they have a certain place within the hierarchy of the organization that is congruent with the job's level of responsibility and complexity and are independent of any concrete worker. Thus, hierarchies and jobs are seen as having no occupants, no human bodies, and thus no gender.

Two of the fundamental components to gendered organizations are the disembodied worker and the job (Acker, 1990). The disembodied worker represents a male whose life centers on his full-time job while a woman takes care of his personal needs. Organizational hierarchies are constructed on gendered processes and the underlying assumptions of the disembodied worker and the job. With these assumptions permeating organizations, masculine attributes pervade work and organizational processes. Acker (2006a) noted that gender inequalities are apparent by "the relative scarcity of women in most top level positions and the existence of large job categories filled almost entirely with low-wage women workers with little power and autonomy" (p. 111). Furthermore, Acker (2006b) observed the need to desist from blaming women for the inequities in organizations. Phillippe and Sullivan (2005) reported that in today's community colleges, women constitute the majority of nonprofessional staff (65 percent), which includes secretaries, clerks, and maintenance. This statistic, coupled with the fact that only 29 percent of community colleges are led by women and the other inequities described, paints the portrait of community colleges as gendered organizations. Given these demographics, Acker's model provides a useful means for better understanding two-year institutions as gendered organizations.

Project Summary

This study analyzed audiotaped and transcribed interviews with six women community college presidents. Each of the women had been leading her institution for less than five years; one participant was serving in her second presidency. Pseudonyms are used to protect the identities of the participants.

To discover more about the gendered nature of community college leadership, a phenomenological research method was employed. Phenomenology research searches for the central underlying meaning of an experience—in this case, the construction by women community college presidents of work within a gendered organization—and uses data reduction to analyze specific statements and themes for possible meanings (Creswell, 1998). This research methodology focuses on how individuals consciously develop meaning through social interactions (Creswell, 1998). We also employed a heuristic lens for deeper interpretation of the experiences described (Van Manen, 1990).

The women leading the campuses in this study did not do so without a context. As noted, 29 percent of all colleges are led by women. The women in the study had spent the majority of their careers working within community colleges. Four of the six ascended to their positions through previous administrative positions, with only two taking the traditional faculty route to a chief academic officer prior to their presidency. All of the women were currently married, whereas only 83 percent of all two-year public community college presidents are married (American Council on Education, 2007).

Cathy Voss is in her first presidency. Previously she held faculty rank at a community college, ultimately moving up to vice president of enrollment services prior to her presidency. Like Voss, Lori Cannon started her career as a faculty member, advancing to department chair, division dean, and vice president of academic affairs prior to her presidency. Maria Smith and Jennifer Cochran started their careers in the K–12 arena. Smith was a curriculum director prior to moving over to community outreach at the community college. She moved from this position to vice president of academic affairs and next to her presidency. Cochran was a high school business teacher, moving over to the community college central office to manage curriculum. She held a central office position in the community college district prior to being tapped by the chancellor of the system to take over as the community college president. Like Cochran, Denise Webster was also tapped by her chancellor for her current presidency. She had been the president of another college in the district prior to this move. Finally, Cindy Hales came to her presidency from the position of dean of students.

Findings

Findings from this research uncovered an organizational structure in community colleges still based on male norms. In particular, the role of the hierarchy and its corresponding reporting structure were present. Although some of the women described their leadership as open and participatory, the hierarchical structure was most apparent. The experiences of these women leaders showcase the types of behaviors that were rewarded as they ascended to the presidency, with links to the disembodied worker inherent in these descriptions.

Embodied Family Life. As the college presidents described their pathways to their current positions, they often noted the serendipitous routes they took along the way. Two of the six women did not pursue a presidency until their husbands retired. Two others intentionally chose their college because of family obligations. The remaining two women worked in a large urban area, giving them increased employment options. Moreover, these latter two were tapped by their male chancellor for their positions, resulting in obtaining presidencies within their district without a formal search or a need to move.

Several of the women noted a defining moment in which they realized they wanted to pursue a presidency. As Voss explained, "I was doing some consulting work with a president who was struggling with his board and was struggling with faculty. He asked me, 'How should I handle this? Would you talk to the board?' And I thought—wow, I could be doing this job!" Fit was of prime concern for her in her search. She visited another institution that was seeking a president but came away thinking it did not feel right.

Since all of the women in the study were married, they had to deal with dual career issues when contemplating a move. One president commented, "Two-academic-career families are hard to find. My husband is a professor of mathematics and retired to come here with me. . . . He got the little spouse tour during the interview." Family played a role for Hales in the move to her current college. She picked the college based on its location and the fit for her family. When the previous president announced his retirement, a male colleague who had been critical of the college indicated to her that he was going to be the next president. Hales reflected, "I tell you, that's enough to take your breath away. And, you know, he had made this announcement to me not even thinking that anybody perhaps in the same leadership team might be interested in being the president too. But in his mind, it was a done deal because he was the man for the job. And then I thought, 'Well, they may not take him, but (they may take someone besides him). And that would be really terrible for the college.'" After conversations with the outgoing president, Hales decided to pursue the presidency herself and ultimately was selected for the position.

Lori Cannon historically made career choices with her family in mind. When her son was a toddler, she was an associate dean. She reflected:

> I decided to get out of it because it was just obvious to me that I wasn't giving my child the attention that he needed. At some point, there are fewer administrative positions at an institution. . . . It was just clear to me at that point when he was just three or four years old that I could not take an administrative position and protect what was important to me, which was the stability of my marriage, my son's growing up in a stable environment. By the time my son was through with college, it was just my husband and me. I thought, I'm not going to spend the rest of my life teaching the same courses every year. So at that point, there was an opportunity to take an interim academic dean position.

The idea of the disembodied worker and male norm of academics worked against Cannon in the choices she made. She did not make a move back to administration until her son was out of college and did not move to her presidency until her husband retired from his academic career.

Smith reflected on the possibility of seeking another presidency: "I consciously made a decision very early on that my first priority would always be my family. . . . If someone offered me a job across the country, I'd love it, but it would take me away from my family. I wouldn't even think about it." Smith had recently been asked to apply for the presidency at a nearby college and opted to pass on the opportunity. She stated, "I just believe that if you do what's right, other opportunities will come, if it should be. Will I ever look for another job? Well, let's put it this way: it's not my career goal, but nothing has ever been my career goal. If something should come up, I would probably take a look at it, but is it my desire to leave? No." The lack of career planning and intentionality for advancement marked Smith's career pathway, as it did many of the other women in the study.

For Cochran and Webster, their presidencies started without a typical search. Instead they were appointed to their positions by the chancellor of the system. Both women had wide experience within the district and the state, making them desirable candidates. As insiders, they were able to enact changes quickly since they did not have to take the time to learn the system. The fact that they could stay within the system meant they did not have to move their families to take a promotion.

Clearly the sequencing of career choices for the women in this study underscores the perpetuation of the disembodied worker in community colleges. The women were all in married relationships, some with children, and they made choices of when to seek advanced positions based on when their lives more mirrored that of their male counterparts: when their children were older or grown and their husband's careers could accommodate the move. This valuing of the public (male) over the private (female) spheres meant the women in the study ultimately had to embrace the male norm in order to secure career advancements.

Getting Tough. Language often serves to reinforce the concept of gender in leadership. West and Zimmerman (1987) refer to "doing gender" as the ideal of societal expectations based on gender. Women are often penalized for acting in ways that are outside what is expected of them. Paradoxically they are at the same time judged against male norms. When gendered organizations value the disembodied employee, the expectations are for women to fit this male-normed mold. One of the presidents told the story of being forceful in her side of an argument and being called a "bitch." She reflected, "I walked out of his office and said, 'I can't work for this man, and what's more, I probably can't work for anyone. I've got to be my own boss.'" Indeed, she was penalized for acting tough outside her gender. Another president, petite in stature, noted that a female board member advised her to wear glasses "to appear more serious." The women needed to act tougher to meet the expected work roles but could not appear too tough.

The women used language that reified their gender, allowing them to support traditional gender roles. Voss reflected, "I spoke in my first convocation that I was particularly well suited to this challenge because we had raised a family on a single faculty member's salary, since I didn't work when our children were young. But I was always pinching pennies and managing—so I was well equipped for this job." Playing to the gender role reified female expectations.

One president stated, "The campus needed somebody who had some strong leadership but also would be willing to be a team player." The notion of the hero leader is embodied in this statement. In order for her to succeed, she needed to be a tough role model. She added, however, that when she walks around campus, "I frighten people." They wonder, "What's she here for?" "What's she looking for?" Her strong persona translated to her negatively perceived campus presence.

Denise Webster reflected on her preparation en route to her presidency: "I've had some experiences where there were institutions that did not want to change—that was a painful lesson, but it was a really good experience that was pretty valuable for me—not comfortable, but boy, you can learn a lot from being in an institution where change is just really rejected as a value." Here the value in the experience was learning how to make the hard decisions that were unpopular.

Working in a Man's World. Emerging definitions of leadership are expanding to be more inclusive of others in locations outside the presidency. Yet research shows that half of the leaders in a recent study indicated their position was why they were a leader (Eddy and VanDerLinden, 2006). Thinking about what it means to be a leader is rooted in self-conceptions of values. The women in this study commented on why they wanted to be a president. For some, it was a realization that they were capable of doing the job, for others it was the fact that they could not work for another person.

The links of leadership to positional power begin to reify the gendered organizational structure of community colleges. Several of the women had mentors who viewed the presidency as a career goal. The support and identification of positional power reinforced the ideal of single leadership, which exemplifies the gendered congruence between responsibility, job complexity, and hierarchical position. Unfortunately, the hierarchy is based on the assumption that leaders can concentrate solely on work because there is someone on the home front supporting the leader. The model of positional leadership as the pinnacle of success begins to leave no alternative role models for women coming up through the ranks of the college. The bind for women is that the quickest route to the upper-level positions is to mirror the practices currently expected, which are based on the disembodied worker.

President Smith followed another woman when she took over her presidency. It was clear the previous president used her position as a stepping-stone. Smith astutely concluded, "I found that kind of hurt me when I came because everyone thought this would be your stepping-stone because you're not old enough [to retire from the college in the near future]." The fact that the women were judged by the actions of the women before them set up a dilemma: not only were they judged by the male norms of organizations, they were measured against what other women prior to them did in the position, which made it difficult to be authentic in their leadership.

Lori Cannon stated frankly, "I know I have the same traits as all presidents do. I want to get things done." What remains implicit in this statement is that these traits are those associated with men, in particular the desire to have a product to show for effort versus typically attributed female traits of working on relationships without a specific measurable outcome. Cannon further noted her aspirations for a presidency. The internal desire to move up in responsibility based on her awareness of her ability to do the job illustrates her increased agency. The desire to be in the position in which the ultimate decisions are made, however, also reifies the male normed hierarchy.

One of the first actions of several of the presidents was to reorganize the hierarchy. In all cases, the changes added structure to the hierarchy and inserted a formal chain of command. The need for additional leadership midway in the hierarchy provided the rationale for these moves. One president commented, "I couldn't get breathing room. I had people at my door constantly!" The addition to the leadership ranks provided a level of protection for the new presidents and served to reinforce the idea of position as the critical factor for leaders.

Cannon discovered challenges facing her college in her first year when the college self-study report was published. She said, "This was the first inclination I've had or intimation that I've had that anything is seriously wrong. And is it my problem? Have I not been sufficiently attentive picking up these signals?" Obviously these problems existed prior to her talking over the helm. The experience affected her to the extent that she decided that if she obtained another presidency, she would request letters of resignation from all senior staff to hold in the event she needed a mechanism to clean house. She learned the need to operate in a more masculine way of leading by this experience. Many of her comments regarding changes she had made since becoming president were done as a means to gain some control. She concluded, "I'll be frank about it: the college has been a real trial. This has been a difficult job." The challenge of being judged against two sets of expectations, the male norms anticipated for the president and acting like a woman while doing this, took their toll.

Breaking Away. Not all elements of these women's presidencies were male influenced. Traditional women's ways of leading were also apparent. These feminized actions, however, still took place within a gendered organization. One president noted that she uses her leadership cabinet to bounce and formulate ideas. However, when she presented concepts to the larger campus, she did so using language of ownership, saying, "This is my plan," versus, "This is our plan." The ideas of others were incorporated, but the framing of them on campus relied on the role of position. She reflected, "I think the challenge for this campus is also to let go of stuff," which inferred that she knew the right direction.

Lori Cannon commented on her disciplinary background and its influence on her, "I'm not a typical physicist either. . . . I think I'm a little more right-brained than that. Maybe it's my femininity that I bring to that. I don't know. But every single one of us is a unique human being with a unique set of past experiences. There probably is no way to plot that out as a model of leader development." Inherent in this reflection is an acknowledgment that things would be different if we acknowledge the feminist side of leading. Also evident was the role of agency in recognizing the role of experience in working toward change and adapting to circumstances in developing as a leader.

The personal ownership of the actions of the president for the college showcases a reliance on relationships, which are often viewed as being woman based. Smith stated, "First of all, when you're a president, if you want to do a really good job, I believe you have to really become part of the institution." Relationships were critical to the women as they took over the helm. Each indicated taking time to get to know campus members and campus issues.

An obvious breaking away of tradition was evident for Denise Webster's campus which was under construction. Webster stated:

> The vision came out of the ability to build a college from scratch in the twenty-first century, taking best practice of everything we all wish we could do but can't because there're always limitations either by organizations or by people you have employed, or by habit, or by physical plant and to really then take full advantage of the opportunity to take the blank page and actually build a learning college.

The ability to start from a blank page allowed for an intentional break from a bureaucratic operation based on male norms and the disembodied worker. The barrier for a full change, however, was apparent even in this situation, since 50 percent of the new employees were hired from within the district. Webster noted, "We hope it will create a situation where there'll be more flexibility and more the ability to react or change—deal with change in less siloed ways to allow us to make those shifts." Still, she commented on the process of creating a new college: "We were encouraged to institute and formulate our organizational structure and really go pretty far out there, away from an academic structure. That's where being in a district limited us." She expanded, "We enjoyed exploring that [different structure], but when it came down to it, this district has vice presidents and deans, and we had to just hire people, have certain things that at least looked like other things in the district."

Conclusion

Community colleges are gendered organizations despite espoused values of being democratic institutions. Reliance on hierarchy and positional power is still evident, as in the creation of a new campus that still used a traditional reporting structure and the move by several of the presidents to add to the organizational hierarchy. The portrait of community colleges with more than a majority of women as students, but less than a third led by women, supports Acker's definition (2006a) of gendered organizations. Mere number increases in women's representation, however, do not address the larger issue of the male-normed organizational structure. Frame-breaking changes to these norms are required to create a gender-neutral institution.

A means of moving forward is the expansion of organizational and leadership research that deconstructs the hegemonic norm of male leadership defining all leadership. Certainly the women presidents represented in this research had expectations foisted on them to act or lead in a particular manner. Indeed, DiCroce (1995) provided a framework for action for women to effect meaningful change in their institutions. She outlined the following actions:

- Break down institutional gender stereotypes.
- Penetrate the institution's power structure, and redefine its sense of power.
- Use the power of office to alter gender-related institutional policy.

- Raise collegial consciousness, and initiate a collegial dialogue on gender.
- Become an active player for public policy development and debate.

Organizationally the chance to build a college from the ground up may provide one means to get beyond the gendered organization. Another option for breaking away from entrenched patterns of behaviors may be through institutional partnerships. Collaborations may provide the basis for a way of rethinking power and leadership roles. For women who have obtained success in their careers to date by acting within the male norms, breaking away from this practice might be impossible since the behavior is ingrained. An increase in personal agency might allow change of these old behaviors.

There are actions that community colleges may take now to facilitate the move to a less gendered organization. The first of these is an acknowledgment that the goals and mission of the organization are not gender neutral, which ultimately will lead to changes in these documents (Ward, 2004). Next, the organization should identify the factors within the community college environment that are contributing to greater gender equality and replicate them throughout the organization (Britton, 2000). Finally, the community college should examine the ways the gendered practices within the organization are rewarded by outside organizations and move toward changing, if not eliminating, this system of compensation for gendered practices.

Research has shown that successful change projects like affirmative action and pay equity campaigns had common characteristics: they targeted a limited set of inequality-producing mechanisms (for instance, hiring practices), combined social movement and legislative support from outside the organization with active support from insiders, and involved coercion or threat of loss (Acker, 2006b). Yet until there is another period of broad social movements supporting organizational change, greater gender equality may be difficult to attain.

The research reported here found that a decade after DiCroce (1995) outlined her action plan of change for women leaders, transformation is still needed. Building on DiCroce's earlier arguments, Kramer (2005) noted, "Although agency may be limited to creating a means to survive within difficult social arrangements, it sometimes produces changes in the environment" (p. 5). Thus, individuals can begin to change the microenvironments within their institutions. Within organizations, power structures still form the basis of the hierarchy, women continue to be judged by male models of leadership, and gendered stereotypes persist. Despite this seemingly discouraging conclusion, this research provides a means of "giving voice to women in order to articulate feminist viewpoints, overturn unitary representations of experience to make way for the multiplicity of not only gender, but race, ethnicity, age, and class" (Hatch and Cunliffe, 2006, p. 275). Recognition of the work remaining to deconstruct gendered organizational structures within community colleges raises the issue to the forefront, offering a forum for dialogue for change and a site for additional research.

References

Acker, J. "Hierarchies, Jobs, Bodies: A Theory of Gendered Organizations." *Gender and Society,* 1990, *4*(2), 139–158.
Acker, J. *Class Questions: Feminist Answers.* Lanham, Md.: Rowman and Littlefield, 2006a.
Acker, J. "Inequality Regimes: Gender, Class, and Race in Organizations." *Gender and Society,* 2006b, *20*(4), 441–464.
American Council on Education. *The American College President.* Washington, D.C.: American Council on Education, 2007.
Amey, M. J., and Twombly, S. B. "Revisioning Leadership in Community Colleges." *Review of Higher Education,* 1992, *15*(2), 125–150.
Britton, D. M. "The Epistemology of the Gendered Organization." *Gender and Society,* 2000, *14*(3), 418–434.
Chliwniak, L. "Higher Education Leadership: Analyzing the Gender Gap." *ASHE-ERIC Higher Education Reports,* 1997, *25*(4), 1–97.
Creswell, J. W. *Qualitative Inquiry and Research Design: Choosing Among Five Traditions.* Thousand Oaks, Calif.: Sage, 1998.
DiCroce, D. M. "Women and the Community College Presidency: Challenges and Possibilities." In B. K. Townsend (ed.), *Gender and Power in the Community College.* New Directions for Community Colleges, no. 89. San Francisco: Jossey-Bass, 1995.
Eddy, P. L., and VanDerLinden, K. "Emerging Definitions of Leadership in Higher Education: New Visions of Leadership or Same Old 'Hero' Leader?" *Community College Review,* 2006, *34*(1), 5–26.
Hatch, M. J., and Cunliffe, A. L. *Organization Theory: Modern, Symbolic, and Postmodern Perspectives.* New York: Oxford University Press, 2006.
Kanter, R. M. *Men and Women of the Corporation.* (2nd ed.) New York: Basic Books, 1993.
Kramer, L. *The Sociology of Gender.* (2nd ed.) Los Angeles: Roxbury Press, 2005.
Monroehurst, R. "Leadership, Women and Higher Education." In H. Eggins (ed.), *Women as Leaders and Managers in Higher Education.* Bristol, Pa.: Society for Research into Higher Education and Open University Press, 1997.
National Center for Education Statistics. *Digest of Education Statistics, 2004.* Washington, D.C.: U.S. Department of Education, 2004.
Phillippe, K. A., and Sullivan, L. G. *National Profile of Community Colleges: Trends and Statistics.* (4th ed.) Washington, D.C.: Community College Press, 2005.
Shults, C. *The Critical Impact of Impending Retirements on Community College Leadership.* Washington, D.C.: American Association of Community Colleges, 2001.
Van Manen, M. *Researching Lived Experience: Human Science for an Action Sensitive Pedagogy.* Albany: State University of New York Press, 1990.
Ward, J. "Not All Differences Are Created Equal: Multiple Jeopardy in a Gendered Organization." *Gender and Society,* 2004, *18*(1), 82–102.
West, C., and Zimmerman, D. H. "Doing Gender." *Gender and Society,* 1987, *1*(2), 125–151.

PAMELA L. EDDY is associate professor in the department of educational leadership at Central Michigan University.

ELIZABETH M. COX is assistant director of the California Community College Collaborative (C4) at the University of California, Riverside.

8

This chapter reports the results of a survey of faculty at one community college in the West. Findings suggest that balancing work and family remains a grave concern for faculty.

Work and Family Balance: How Community College Faculty Cope

Margaret W. Sallee

Over the past decade, work-family balance policies have become a popular recruitment tool for research universities. In an effort to recruit and retain faculty, these institutions offer an array of policies, including time off for the birth of a child, the opportunity to stop the tenure clock, and a temporary reduction in teaching duties. Although institutions typically focus on providing accommodations to new parents, faculty cope with a range of demands throughout the life cycle. The need for accommodations does not stop after the arrival of a new child in the home. Many faculty report needing additional time off due to a child or partner's illness. As the professoriate ages, so do their parents. Many older professors now seek accommodations not for the birth of a child, but to provide care to their aging parents.

Although work-family balance policies are slowly becoming the norm at four-year institutions, they are not equally common at community colleges. In part, this discrepancy is due to the cost of providing assistance to faculty. Unlike community colleges, research institutions tend to have sufficient resources to offer accommodations for faculty, such as a paid release from teaching duties. However, community colleges can implement a range of work-family balance initiatives that cost the institution little and provide assistance to faculty. Although research institutions are at the forefront of the work-family balance movement in academe, community colleges need not simply adopt identical policies and practices. As I will discuss, community college faculty members spend considerably more time on teaching responsibilities and are more likely to be employed part

NEW DIRECTIONS FOR COMMUNITY COLLEGES, no. 142, Summer 2008
Published online in Wiley InterScience (www.interscience.wiley.com) • DOI: 10.1002/cc.327

time than their four-year-institution counterparts. Given these significant differences, community colleges should develop policies that address the unique needs of their faculty. In this chapter, I present the results of an exploratory study of the availability of policies and faculty satisfaction at one community college.

The Busy Life of a Faculty Member

Faculty members face many demands on their time. They are expected to teach, meet with students, serve on committees, attend department meetings, and in some cases conduct research. All faculty members face a multitude of demands on their time outside campus. Faculty may have spouses or partners, children, parents, extended family, or friends who require various degrees of care. However, the majority of institutional accommodations focus on providing assistance to faculty members with children. Yet today's faculty members may find themselves spending just as much time caring for their parents as they do for their children.

Although faculty members of both genders may worry about balancing work and family, the burden remains much greater for women as they spend more time performing household duties and tending to children than men do. In their survey of forty-four hundred ladder-rank faculty, Mason and Goulden (2004) found that women with children spend over one hundred hours a week on caregiving, housework, and professional responsibilities, while men spend closer to eighty-five hours a week on the same tasks. Of particular interest, men and women reported spending nearly equal time on professional responsibilities and housework. The largest discrepancy arises in time spent with children: women reported spending 35.5 hours a week with their children, while men spent 20.3 hours with their children. Women spend nearly twice the amount of time with their children as men yet still spend essentially the same amount of time fulfilling professional responsibilities.

The majority of institutional policies and research literature focus on the needs of parents. However, an increasing number of middle-aged faculty members find themselves providing care for their own aging parents. According to the Older Women's League (2001), 31 percent of the adult American population provides some sort of informal care for friends or relatives over the age of fifty. Furthermore, 20 to 40 percent are members of the sandwich generation, caring for both children and aging parents. Much like child rearing responsibilities, elder care disproportionately falls to women (Doress-Worters, 1994). One estimate suggests that 75 percent of all elder care is performed by women (Older Women's League, 2001).

Although women perform the majority of care work, this does not suggest that achieving a work-family balance is not a concern for men. Part of women's increased responsibility in the home comes from societal expectations and institutional policies that penalize men for engaging in family care. Although few studies have examined the role of fathers in academic settings, research in corporate environments found cultures that ranged from discouraging to hostile to men who prioritize family over career (Halverson, 2003; Malin, 1998). However, as Mason and Goulden's study (2004) indicates, men perform housework and child care in the home. Perhaps if institutional policies provided greater incentive, their involvement would approach that of women.

Institutional Support: How Colleges and Universities Are Responding

Over the past two decades, an increasing number of colleges and universities have introduced an array of family-friendly policies to help faculty members balance the competing demands of their lives. Given the fact that men have historically dominated the ranks of the faculty at four-year institutions, the introduction of such policies grew out of efforts to recruit and retain female faculty. Initial policies tended to provide paid maternity leave to female faculty members, with little recognition given to men's roles. Over the past decade, institutions have expanded the availability of policies to faculty of both genders. Despite these gains, not all institutions provide the same types of policies. In a survey of 255 higher education institutions, Hollenshead and colleagues (2005) identified seven types of accommodations that might be available at different institutions:

- Paid leave after childbirth
- Paid dependent care leave
- Unpaid dependent care leave
- A break in the tenure clock
- Modified duties
- Reduced, part-time, and job-share appointments
- Staff assistance with work-family policy

With the exception of paid leave to recover from childbirth, all of these policies can be available to faculty of either gender, though institutions do not necessarily offer them on a gender-neutral basis. Some institutions rely on traditional notions of parenting roles. Despite the fact that both men and women juggle competing responsibilities at home and work, some institutions continue to offer accommodations to women only. In doing so, these institutions perpetuate outdated gender roles, disadvantaging women in the workplace and men who want to be involved fathers.

Using the 1994 Carnegie classification of institutional types, Hollenshead and colleagues (2005) compared the availability of policies across institutions. They found that research institutions offered 2.99 policies per campus, while community colleges offered 0.80 policies per campus. Of the thirty community colleges surveyed, 50 percent offered no policies for faculty use and 37 percent offered only one of the policies.

Of the seven types of accommodations listed, community colleges were most likely to offer unpaid leave beyond the Family and Medical Leave Act. Forty-three percent of surveyed institutions had a formal policy in place, and an additional 10 percent had informal policies. The second most popular policy at community colleges is that of reduced appointment for ordinary needs. Seven percent of institutions offered such a formal policy, though an additional 17 percent reported that informal arrangements could be made to accommodate the requests of faculty (Hollenshead and others, 2005). Although informal policies offer faculty members the opportunity to make arrangements to meet their needs, they are less preferable than formal policies. Informal policies often depend on the goodwill of the department chair, who can play a critical role in creating a supportive climate (Quinn, Lange, and Olswang, 2004; Sullivan, Hollenshead, and Smith, 2004; Waltman and August, 2005). Not all department chairs are amenable to helping faculty balance their competing demands.

Of the remaining policies, no more than 7 percent of the institutions offered any of the accommodations. This is in marked contrast to the practices of research institutions. For example, 86 percent of research institutions have formal policies to stop the tenure clock. In contrast, only 7 percent of community colleges offered the same formal policy (Hollenshead and others, 2005). In part, this difference may be due to the different requirements of earning tenure at a research institution versus a community college, an issue to which I return shortly.

The Needs of Community College Faculty

Two- and four-year institutions have nearly opposite hiring patterns. Two out of three faculty members at four-year institutions are employed full time. In contrast, two out of three faculty members are part time at community colleges. As such, the types of accommodation that the institution must provide to employees differ considerably. When institutions provide accommodations to their faculty members, they are often geared toward full-time employees. However, many part-time faculty members are employed at multiple community colleges in an attempt to piece together full-time work. Although these faculty members work full time, they rarely receive assistance in balancing their competing demands.

Unlike faculty at four-year institutions, community college faculty are primarily teachers. Full-time community college faculty members spend 89 percent of their time on teaching-related responsibilities (National Center for Education Statistics, 2005). Though faculty may find their work fulfilling, the demands of full-time teaching place additional stress on those who need to take leave. For example, in their study of thirty female junior faculty members at twelve community colleges, Wolf-Wendel, Ward, and Twombly (2007) found that the greatest stress in juggling their work and home lives came from finding colleagues to cover classes, particularly after the birth of a child. Efforts to provide assistance to community college faculty need to account for the explicit focus on teaching. In addition, community college faculty are more likely to be represented by unions than their four-year counterparts are. While unions generally play a critical role in negotiating salary and other benefits, the earlier review of the availability of leave policies suggests that unions for community college faculty have yet to make work-family balance issues a focus of their advocacy.

Despite the amount of time that community college faculty devote to teaching, several studies suggest that faculty choose to work at community colleges out of a desire to achieve a balance between their personal and professional lives (Townsend and LaPaglia, 2000; Wolf-Wendel, Ward, and Twombly, 2007). In fact, Wolf-Wendel, Ward, and Twombly (2007) found that despite the challenges of teaching, the majority of faculty in their study were satisfied with their positions and found that they were able to teach while simultaneously raising a family. However, their findings stand in contrast to those of this survey in which faculty reported feeling a lack of support from their institution.

A Work-Life Survey: The Case of One Institution

Given the dearth of literature on work-life balance issues for community college faculty, this exploratory study provides basic information on some of the challenges for this population. I developed a twenty-item survey seeking to ascertain faculty members' awareness of the availability of policies at their institution, measure their satisfaction with their work-life balance, and collect key demographic variables. Although most questions offered fixed responses, two questions asked respondents to comment on ways their institution currently helps and might better help faculty achieve a work-life balance. Responses to both types of questions are reported here.

Site Selection. The survey was administered to faculty at Meadowland College (a pseudonym), a community college located in a metropolitan area on the West Coast. Meadowland College is a member of the Nature Valley Community College District, a consortium of four two-year institutions. The college enrolls approximately thirty-three thousand full-time and part-time students. In addition to offering courses at its main campus, the college operates four satellite centers in the greater metropolitan area. The college employs approximately twelve hundred full-time and part-time faculty and staff.

Sample. The survey was administered online. An e-mail was sent to the faculty listserv explaining the study and including a link to the survey site. Initial contact yielded fifty survey responses. Two weeks later, a follow-up reminder was sent, yielding an additional thirty-nine responses. In total, eighty-nine faculty members completed the survey.

Of the eighty-nine faculty members who responded to the survey, fifty-four were women, twenty-eight were men, and seven declined to state their gender. In addition, seventeen were employed at the institution part time while sixty-six were employed full time. Although Meadowland College uses a high number of adjunct faculty, survey respondents were overwhelmingly employed full time. Respondents also ranged in age. Nine respondents were under the age of thirty-five, forty-one were between thirty-five and fifty, and thirty-three were over the age of fifty. The demographics of respondents differ slightly from the national profile of community college faculty discussed earlier. Survey respondents were far more likely to be full-time and more likely to be female than the typical faculty member. This profile—predominantly female, predominantly full time, and older—may help explain responses to the survey.

Findings

Results of the survey suggest that faculty feel overworked and undervalued by the institution. As in previous studies, many Meadowland faculty members reported that they chose to work at a community college to better integrate their personal and professional lives. Seventy-two percent of respondents indicated that their decision to work at a community college was motivated, in some part, by a desire to balance their personal and professional lives. Despite consciously seeking a balanced work environment, many faculty reported conflicts among their multiple responsibilities. Eighty-four percent of respondents indicated that they frequently feel that they have to choose between their home and work lives.

Part of this conflict may stem from a lack of perceived support from both the institution and individual departments. Only 17 percent of respondents agreed or strongly agreed that the college encourages faculty to balance their home and work lives. On a scale of 1 to 5, where 1 is highly unsupportive and 5 is highly supportive, the mean faculty score for this item was 2.64. Faculty viewed their own departments as marginally more supportive. Whereas the mean score for the institution as a whole was 2.64, the mean score for department climate was 3.13.

Forty-seven percent of respondents indicated that they were unaware of the existence of any institutional work-life policy or program. However, such programs clearly exist: 19 percent of respondents indicated that they had used such policies. Faculty responses suggest that the institution has failed to adequately promote the availability of such policies. This failure to disseminate information may in part account for faculty members' dissatisfaction with the level of support received from the campus as a whole.

Concerns and Desires of Faculty. Eighty-three percent of respondents indicated that at least one major life event had been a concern in the previous three years. Although most work-life policies focus on providing relief due to the arrival of a child, only 17 percent of respondents indicated that they had recently experienced the arrival of a new child. The majority of life events reported concerned illness or caring for aging parents. Twenty-three percent of respondents indicated that they had experienced a significant illness in the previous three years, 18 percent indicated that a partner or child had experienced a significant illness, and 34 percent indicated that they had engaged in elder care. Self-selection bias may explain these unusually high percentages of respondents experiencing significant illness. Faculty who have experienced significant stresses on their personal lives may have been more likely to complete the survey. Although birth and child care were significant issues for some of the faculty, the results indicate that faculty members face a variety of issues throughout their lives that could benefit from additional support from the institution.

Due to federal laws like the 1978 Pregnancy Discrimination Act, institutions typically provide support to pregnant employees. Forty-one (46 percent) of respondents indicated that they had experienced the arrival of a new child during their employment at the institution. Survey results indicated that women used a variety of policies related to the birth of a child and some in combination. Six women were able to rely on formal maternity leave policies, fourteen women used sick leave, eleven women took unpaid leave, and two women took no leave at all. In their open-ended responses, some women indicated frustration with the lack of availability of leave policies. One faculty member wrote, "Can you call one day 'maternity leave'? My union has only negotiated one day of maternity leave! My husband got more official paternity leave than I got maternity leave!" Another faculty member commented, "As a part-timer, the only option in more than thirty years for anything related to a leave request has been unpaid with a good risk of no job or a different assignment upon return." Although leave policies may exist, they provide no financial compensation and, for part-time faculty, no job protection, thereby making it impossible for some women to take leave.

Respondents were asked to rate which policies and provisions they would like to see their institution provide. Respondents were most eager for the institution to offer on-site child care to faculty. Sixty-three percent of respondents rated child care as a priority. Fifty-two percent of respondents indicated that they would like the campus to offer a reduction in teaching duties following the birth of a child. And 46 percent expressed interest in the opportunity to stop the tenure clock due to the birth of a child. Although there was no consensus on which policies the institution should provide, nearly all faculty indicated that the campus should provide at least some assistance to faculty. Only five participants (6 percent) responded that the institution should not provide any assistance to faculty.

Open-Ended Responses. Two questions allowed respondents to comment on ways the campus encourages faculty to achieve a work-life balance and the ways in which the campus might improve their efforts. On the whole, faculty had difficulty identifying exemplary programs, though they generated a lengthy list of ways the institution might intervene.

What the Campus Does Well. Fifty-one faculty members described policies and practices already in place at Meadowland College. Responses are divided into six broad topical areas. By far, the largest group of respondents indicated that the campus did not offer any policies or programs to promote work-life balance. Twenty-one respondents indicated either that they had no knowledge of such policies or that the campus did not offer any policies. An additional three respondents argued that providing such programs and policies was not an institutional responsibility.

Other respondents highlighted several ways the campus attends to the needs of faculty. Seven respondents commented that the campus provided workshops on a range of topics, including coping with stress and dealing with aging parents. One respondent's comments sum up the challenges that many faculty members seemed to express: "As far as I know, the main or only program is a monthly support group. I've seen the promotions for it—but don't have time to attend!" Two respondents indicated that there were a limited number of spaces available in the on-campus child care centers, which are primarily designated for student use. However, for the majority of faculty, available campus child care is lacking.

The workshops and child care were the only two initiatives that faculty members identified. Remaining comments pointed to informal arrangements that eased efforts to balance responsibilities. Eight respondents commented on flexible scheduling patterns in terms of assigning class times in consideration of family obligations and in terms of being able to work from home. Two respondents commented that while the campus as a whole is not supportive of achieving a work-life balance, deans and department chairs were occasionally willing to provide additional support. However, when such assistance is not institutionalized, it runs the risk of disappearing with a change in leadership.

Room for Improvement. More respondents commented on programs and policies they would like to see Meadowland College offer. Sixty-two faculty provided suggestions that can be grouped into seven areas. Eighteen faculty members highlighted work-related responsibilities. For example, some commented on understaffing of both faculty and administrative staff. One respondent, who works at one of the satellite centers, indicated that she spends a majority of her time performing janitorial and administrative functions because there is no one else to do them. Other respondents commented on a need to reduce the standard course load or for release time in recognition of completion of other duties, such as advising or being chair of a department. Others suggested that the campus also provide release time for professional development, such as learning new technologies or pedagogies. The overwhelming tone of responses indicates that faculty feel overworked and unsupported by campus administration.

Faculty also identified a variety of programs that Meadowland might offer. Seven respondents suggested that the administration should focus on disseminating information about existing leave policies. Some recommended that the campus establish an office that focuses on explaining these policies. Others suggested holding workshops, both to review existing policies and to focus on particular issues, such as the stress and elder care workshops. As responses to other questions suggest, the campus administration has failed to adequately promote its policies to all constituencies on campus.

Faculty members also wrote of the need to establish child care on campus. Seven respondents suggested that the campus provide slots for faculty and staff children rather than only students' children. Others wrote of a general desire to make the campus more family friendly. Several respondents wrote at length about the ways in which campus responsibilities encroach on their familial responsibilities. For example, one faculty member wrote, "Simply recognizing that faculty have the same twenty-four hours per day limitations and that the college is not entitled to ALL twenty-four hours each day. Administration sometimes expects or demands commitment beyond the contract hours." This faculty member expresses frustration that administrators expect employees to allow their work responsibilities to encroach on their home time but have not made any provisions to blend home responsibilities with work.

Eight respondents wrote about the need to offer additional leave policies, ranging from providing paid maternity leave to a reduction in teaching duties following the birth of a child. In addition to formal leave policies, nine respondents suggested a variety of other programs, including establishing spousal hiring programs, the ability to job-share when children are young, and introducing a flexible work week to allow faculty to teach the same number of classes on a reduced number of days.

Three part-time faculty members commented that they tend to be neglected by the campus. One faculty member suggested improving medical benefits and sick pay for adjuncts who had provided a certain amount of consistent service. Another asked for the same consideration (office space, pay, benefits) given to full-time faculty. A third suggested that the campus follow the lead of research institutions by creating full-time, non-tenure-track positions: "If my college(s) established a full-time, non-tenure-track position, part-time faculty could carry the same work load without having the additional stress of working in different counties and different schools." Part-time faculty members who work at multiple institutions are those most in need of policies to help them achieve a balanced life, yet they are unlikely to be the target of institutional efforts.

As survey responses indicate, community college faculty have far fewer resources to draw on than their university counterparts. The college offers little assistance to encourage faculty to achieve a work-family balance. Faculty in the sample feel unsupported by their institution, and many were unaware of the limited resources, such as a workshop series, that the campus provided. Many faculty commented on the need for paid leave for major life events; some simply wanted unpaid release time with the promise of a position on return. Although all institutions of higher education employ adjunct instructors, the practice is becoming the norm at community colleges. Yet part-time instructors receive the least assistance from the institution.

Suggestions for Practice

As the results of the survey indicate, community college faculty do not have access to many work-life policies and programs. Although most research institutions have programs for faculty, community colleges should not simply adopt these same practices. Rather, policies and programs should be tailored to fit the unique needs of community college faculty. I conclude by offering five suggestions for institutions interested in promoting a family-friendly climate on campus:

- *Establish a central site for information.* Although Meadowland offered few programs for faculty, survey responses indicated that many faculty did not know of their existence. Campuses should widely disseminate information about programs and policies. Institutions might consider establishing a central Web site that contains information not only about benefits but also about upcoming workshops and other events that are designed to promote a work-family balance.
- *Establish programs that are not resource intensive.* While institutions might work toward establishing programs such as a release from teaching duties following the birth of a child, they can also offer a variety of non-resource-intensive programs and policies. For example, colleges might offer an unpaid leave of absence in excess of the Family and Medical Leave Act. Unpaid leave would allow faculty members to attend to critical personal matters and be assured of their position on their return. In addition, institutions might offer monthly workshops on topics such as managing stress, performing elder care, breast-feeding, and physical and mental health. As survey responses made clear, programs should focus on issues throughout the faculty life cycle, ranging from caring for children to caring for parents.
- *Include part-time faculty members.* Results from this survey suggest that many part-time faculty members feel overworked and close to burnout. Given that the majority of faculty members at community colleges across the nation are employed part time, they deserve access to work-family balance resources. Institutions might consider offering additional benefits to part-time faculty members who have been employed by the institution for a particular length of time.
- *Implement programs that address faculty members' greatest responsibility.* Community colleges should focus on reconciling teaching demands with responsibilities in the home. Institutions might consider offering sabbaticals to faculty, both as a chance for personal renewal and to allow them to learn additional pedagogies. Colleges should also consider how to assist faculty who unexpectedly need to miss class. Institutions might consider creating a campuswide system that allows faculty members to find substitutes for their courses.
- *Develop programs with the needs of faculty in mind.* Although Meadowland faculty identified a number of issues that they would like to see ad-

dressed, each campus has different strengths and different needs. Institutions might consider conducting a simple Web-based survey using an online site such as Survey Monkey to identify the needs of their faculty.

These suggestions will not work for all institutions. Some might balk at providing additional accommodations for part-time faculty, arguing that they lack the resources to do so. Although funding will always be an issue, faculty members are the core resource of every community college. As the survey results indicate, community college faculty need some assistance with achieving a balance between their personal and professional lives. These suggestions focus on interventions in the workplace—providing assistance with locating substitutes, offering workshops—and in the home—providing unpaid leave to full- and part-time faculty.

References

Doress-Worters, P. B. "Adding Elder Care to Women's Multiple Roles: A Critical Review of the Caregiver Stress and Multiple Role Literatures." *Sex Roles,* 1994, *31*(9–10), 597–616.

Halverson, C. "From Here to Paternity: When Men Are Not Taking Paternity Leave Under the Family and Medical Leave Act." *Wisconsin Women's Law Journal,* 2003, *18,* 257–279.

Hollenshead, C. S., and others. "Work-Family Policies in Higher Education: Survey Data and Case Studies of Policy Implementation." In J. W. Curtis (ed.), *The Challenge of Balancing Faculty Careers and Family Work.* New Directions for Higher Education, no. 120. San Francisco: Jossey-Bass, 2005.

Malin, M. H. "Fathers and Parental Leave Revisited." *Northern Illinois University Law Review,* 1998, *19,* 25–56.

Mason, M. A., and Goulden, M. "Do Babies Matter (Part II)? Closing the Baby Gap." *Academe,* 2004, *90*(6), 10–15.

National Center for Education Statistics. *2004 National Study of Postsecondary Faculty Report on Faculty and Instructional Staff.* Washington, D.C.: U.S. Department of Education, 2005.

Older Women's League. *Faces of Caregiving.* Washington, D.C.: Older Women's League, 2001.

Quinn, K., Lange, S. E., and Olswang, S. G. "Family-Friendly Policies and the Research University." *Academe,* 2004, *90*(6), 32–34.

Sullivan, B., Hollenshead, C., and Smith, G. "Developing and Implementing Work-Family Policies for Faculty." *Academe,* 2004, *90*(6), 24–27.

Townsend, B. K., and LaPaglia, N. "Are We Marginalized Within Academe? Perceptions of Two-Year College Faculty." *Community College Review,* 2000, *28*(1), 41–48.

Waltman, J., and August, L. *Tenure Clock, Modified Duties, and Sick Leave Policies: Creating a Network of Support and Understanding for University of Michigan Faculty During Pregnancy and Childbirth.* Ann Arbor: Center for the Education of Women, University of Michigan, 2005.

Wolf-Wendel, L., Ward, K., and Twombly, S. B. "Faculty Life at Community Colleges: The Perspective of Women with Children." *Community College Review,* 2007, *34*(4), 255–281.

MARGARET W. SALLEE is a doctoral candidate and research assistant in the Center for Higher Education Policy Analysis at the University of Southern California.

9

This chapter applies the new 2005 Carnegie Basic Classifications to analyze gender equity issues at community colleges using Equity and Athletic Disclosure Act data. Gender inequities were observed, and suggestions are offered to create more gender-friendly practices and improve compliance with Title IX.

Meeting the Challenge of Gender Equity in Community College Athletics

Cindy Castañeda, Stephen G. Katsinas, David E. Hardy

Title IX of the Education Amendments of 1972 state, "No person in the United States shall, on the basis of sex, be excluded from participation in, be denied the benefits of, or be subjected to discrimination under any education program or activity receiving federal financial assistance" (U.S. Department of Education, 2003, n.p.). This provision paved the way for student-initiated lawsuits claiming discrimination in the area of intercollegiate athletics and resulted in a great expansion in opportunities for women and girls to participate in athletics.

Thirty-six years after the passage of Title IX, it seems reasonable to assess the status of gender equity in intercollegiate athletics. A substantial body of scholarly books and articles exists on the subject at four-year colleges and universities. Interestingly enough, little work explores two-year colleges. To address this deficiency, this chapter draws from a variety of sources. Our primary source is Castañeda's 2004 dissertation, which used data from the Equity and Athletic Disclosure Act (EADA) and the National Center for Education Statistics' Integrated Postsecondary Education Data System (IPEDS) to analyze gender equity in three compliance areas critical for assessing Title IX: compliance and accommodation of student interest and ability, athletic financial assistance, and other program areas such as coaching and recruitment. To further illuminate gender equity issues, the 2005 Basic Classifications of Institutions of Higher Education from the Carnegie

NEW DIRECTIONS FOR COMMUNITY COLLEGES, no. 142, Summer 2008 © 2008 Wiley Periodicals, Inc.
Published online in Wiley InterScience (www.interscience.wiley.com) • DOI: 10.1002/cc.328

Foundation (2006) are used to highlight differences and similarities among and between types of community colleges.

The chapter begins with a literature review, a description of Castañeda's methodology, and a presentation of data related to gender equity. It concludes with suggestions for improved policy and practice to promote better compliance with Title IX and more equitable community college athletic programs.

Literature Review

The role of intercollegiate athletics in colleges has received increased scrutiny in recent years (Thelin, 1994; Telander, 1996). Little of the attention has been positive. Concerns with the graduation rates of athletes, the balance of academics and athletics, governance and oversight issues, and inappropriate inducements made by athletics supporters have been the areas of greatest concern. Attention from the media, academics, foundations, and the Congress has almost exclusively focused on reforming Division I of the National Collegiate Athletic Association (NCAA). These include various reports by the American Association of University Professors (2002), the Knight Commission on Intercollegiate Athletics (Dempsey, 2002), and the U.S. General Accounting Office (2007).

The literature on community college participation in intercollegiate athletics and gender equity in community colleges is small. Koos's *The Junior College Movement* (1925) found "each of the four divisions of activities—athletic, literary, musical, social and religious—shows an increase from the smallest to the largest junior colleges, an increase reflected in the average total numbers [of groups or teams]" (1925, p. 183). Medsker's *The Junior College: Profile and Prospects* (1960) made no mention of athletics. Two of the four college profiles in Fields's (1962) *The Community College Movement* referenced athletics. Thornton's *The Community Junior College* (1972) identified intercollegiate athletics as a special student activity "because of their inherent attraction for many junior college students as participants and as spectators and because of their appeal to the public at large" (p. 274). The author added, "For women, too, the lessons of sportsmanship are important and should be encouraged by appropriate *intramural* competition in suitable sports" (p. 274). Cohen and Brawer's fourth edition of *The American Community College* (2003) mentioned athletics twice, suggesting the reduction of athletics as a possible cost control strategy and in reference to student services. "Athletic programs are presumptively planned so that student athletes can enjoy the benefits of extracurricular activity along with their academic programs" (p. 209).

The benefits of college athletics has been discussed by various authors. Some propose that athletics primarily aids individual student development. Others champion athletics as being essential to the mission of a comprehensive community college and promotion of school spirit and overall reputation of a college. The internal benefits at the student level include individual student development, access to college, and availability of supporting activities such as band, cheerleading, and dance or drill teams. Thornton (1972), Bennion (1992), and Campbell (1988) all note that intercollegiate athletics provides opportunities for students who might not otherwise be able to attend college. Gerdy (1997) acknowledges this concept but views the community college role more skeptically: "High school prospects who fail to meet NCAA initial eligibility standards are farmed out to junior colleges and after two years of usually suspect academic remediation are admitted to four-year institutions as transfers" (p. 142). In contrast, for Monroe (1972), the benefits of student activities were evident and indisputable: "Innumerable students poorly motivated in academic areas become motivated sufficiently to remain eligible for participation in athletics or some other activity" (p. 43). However, Monroe offered no evidence to support these broad claims. Others note that athletics can provide socializing, leadership, and sportsmanship opportunities for participants (Thornton, 1972; Bennion, 1992). Stokes (1979) concluded that athletics "must have as their end, human development" (p. 432).

Internal benefits for community colleges with intercollegiate athletics include increased full-time enrollment, school spirit (Bennion, 1992; Pollock and Pingley, 1986), and potentially new revenue, with enhancement of the college environment as a by-product (Campbell, 1988). Stokes (1979) argued that sports "provide a rallying point and help students develop pride in their institutions" (p. 432).

External and intangible benefits associated with community college involvement in athletics include enhanced publicity (Smith, 1987; Campbell, 1988; Berson, 1996; Pollock and Pingley, 1986), goodwill, and community linkages. However, Fink and Kirk (1979) caution, "If community college athletics programs are designed and administered to build public relations, student morale, and alumni loyalty, then the problems of large institutions may be duplicated. The focus will no longer be on the athlete but on the event and the fans" (p. 440). Others express concern over a perceived inherent contradiction between the philosophy of universal access and having selective athletic teams. Campion (1990) contended that limiting the size of athletic teams was contradictory to the community college cornerstone of open participation. In addition, Fink and Kirk (1979) argued that athletics available only to the talented few went against the mission of open access grounding community colleges. They advocated opening participation for men and women on the same teams whenever possible. Others argue that athletes should be recruited from and receive aid only if they live inside the college's designated service area (Steiner and Milander, 1978) and said that recruiting outside the service area runs contrary to the community-centered mission of the colleges. Stokes (1979) asked presidents to consider, "Should a policy of limiting scholarships to the geographic area of the college be established? Are there educational reasons to recruit in other states?" (p. 436).

Turning to gender equity, Gavora's *Tilting the Playing Field: Schools, Sports, Sex, and Title IX* (2002) includes but one community college in its index. The only two publications identified in the literature were both focused specifically on California (Owiesny, 2000; RMC Corporation, 2004). Owiesny found gender equity had not been achieved, findings corroborated by RMC in its report for the California Postsecondary Education Commission: "Community colleges' greatest gender disparity in athletics was in the area of participation. In fact, only 8 percent of the 91 responding community colleges were in compliance with Title IX based on proportionality—that is, had participation rates that were within five percentage points of the enrollment rates for each gender—and 84 percent were considerably outside the range of acceptability" (p. xi). RMC and Owiesny also found inequities in the number of male and female coaches, athletic directors, and average numbers of coaches per men's and women's teams.

Methodology

To assess gender equity in intercollegiate athletics at community colleges, Castañeda (2004) conducted a national census of intercollegiate athletics at U.S. community colleges using data furnished by the institutions to the federal government through EADA, which was passed in 1994 and incorporated into the 1996 Higher Education Act Reauthorization. The EADA requires "co-educational institutions of postsecondary education that participate in a Title IV, federal student financial assistance program, and have an intercollegiate athletic program, to prepare an annual report to the Department of Education on athletic participation, staffing, and revenues and expenses, by men's and women's teams" (U.S. Department of Education, 2004).

The EADA survey data were first collected online in 2001 and are available at the U.S. Department of Education's Web site. The data include the number and types of sports and students on each team; athletic scholarships by gender, race, and sport; and revenue and expenditure data. Colleges wishing to receive federal funds are required to respond; just eighteen colleges with intercollegiate athletics did not submit EADA surveys for 2002–2003.

Castañeda requested and received the 2002–2003 and 2003–2004 EADA survey data directly from the U.S. Department of Education. These were then connected to the classification codes of associate degree colleges from the Carnegie 2005 Basic Classifications, matching the unique six-digit institution code assigned by the U.S. Department of Education. While the 2005 Basic Classifications include eleven types of associate colleges, our

Table 9.1. Unduplicated Head Count of Students Participating in Intercollegiate Athletics at U.S. Community Colleges, 2001–2002, by Gender and 2005 Carnegie Basic Institutional Classification

	Female Athletes		*Male Athletes*		*Total Athletes*
Carnegie Classification	*Number*	*%*	*Number*	*%*	*Number*
Rural small	1,661	34	3,249	66	4,910
Rural medium	6,262	37	10,856	63	17,118
Rural large	4,588	39	7,245	61	11,833
Rural total	12,511	37	21,350	63	33,861
Suburban single campus	4,584	37	7,843	63	12,427
Suburban multicampus	3,948	37	6,760	63	10,708
Suburban total	8,532	37	14,603	63	23,135
Urban single	1,015	37	1,765	63	2,780
Urban multicampus	4,640	36	8,142	64	12,782
Urban total	5,655	36	9,907	64	15,562
Grand total	26,698	37	45,860	63	72,558

Note: Percentages may not add to 100 percent due to rounding. Includes students who do not receive athletic-related aid.

focus was on the geographically based categories (urban, suburban, and rural associate colleges) (Castañeda, 2004).

Student Interest and Ability

One area of compliance under Title IX is the accommodation of student interest and ability. The results in this area are mixed. In 2002–2003, there were nearly equal numbers of intercollegiate athletics teams for women and for men, 558 (48.7 percent) versus 565 (51.3 percent), respectively. The average number of sports per college was 3.8 for women and 4.0 for men. Yet the participation by individuals was skewed heavily toward males (Castañeda, 2004). Table 9.1 shows that 72,558 student athletes participated in college-sponsored intercollegiate athletics in that year; only 37 percent were females (Castañeda, 2004). Whether the disparity in athletic participation was reflective of student interest, age distribution, or opportunity to participate in intercollegiate teams is unclear.

It is not possible to ascertain from the EADA data set whether the athletic offerings met student interests and needs. However, it is possible to comment on whether the first method of demonstrating Title IX compliance, by providing opportunities that are substantially proportional to the rates of full-time, degree seeking students, was met. When compared to the percentage of full-time, degree-seeking students, the proportion of female athletes is not aligned. Women accounted for 55 percent of all full-time degree-seeking students enrolled at colleges that offered athletics in 2002–2003, yet only 37 percent of the athletes were female in 2001–2002 (Castañeda, 2004). Direct data year comparisons were unavailable due to the staggered nature of IPEDS and EADA surveys.

Achieving gender equity in participation is an even greater challenge at community colleges fielding football teams. Colleges that offered football had an even lower participation by women athletes, barely reaching 30 percent. By contrast, women accounted for an average of 42 percent of athletes at community colleges that did not offer football (Castañeda, 2004).

Athletes accounted for a higher percentage of full-time students at rural community colleges as compared to suburban or urban community colleges. At the high end, athletes accounted for 16 percent of full-time degree-seeking students at small rural colleges and a low of only 4 percent of students at urban, single-campus colleges (Castañeda, 2004). Castañeda estimates that an average of 5.3 percent and 10.9 percent of full-time degree- and certificate-seeking women and men at public community colleges, respectively, were student athletes. Since this study was not longitudinal, changes in levels of participation by women could not be observed. However, the growth in membership in the National Junior College Athletics Association (NJCAA) of 8 percent, or forty colleges, can be inferred as trending toward expanding opportunities (Ashburn, 2007).

Athletic-Related Financial Assistance

Table 9.2 shows the clear attempts by community colleges to achieve gender equity as it relates to athletic financial assistance, with women receiving 44 percent of the over $47 million awarded in 2003–2004. Females received 42 percent of athletic aid compared to 58 percent for males, although women account for only 37 percent of all athletes. The fact that women accounted for 42 percent of all athletes receiving athletic aid and had a higher average scholarship amount than men by nearly $300 provides strong evidence of efforts by community colleges to comply with Title IX.

As Table 9.3 indicates, the average number of athletic scholarships awarded by U.S. community colleges is seventy-four, with thirty-one to women and forty-four to men (Castañeda, 2004). The average of total dollars spent per college on athletic-related aid was $142,899 in 2002–2003, with a high for large rural colleges at just under $200,000, and a low of $84,422 for suburban single-campus colleges. The average athletic aid award for female and male athletes nationally was $2,038 and $1,816, respectively, with very limited variation by community college type (Castañeda, 2004). Overall, 63 percent of colleges offering athletics had at least one sport in which partial scholarships could have been offered. The sports with the greatest availability of athletic scholarships to women were basketball, softball, volleyball, soccer, and tennis.

Table 9.2. Athletic Aid Recipients and Average Amount in Athletic Aid Awarded at Community Colleges, by Gender and 2005 Carnegie Basic Classification, 2003–2004

	Athletic Aid Recipients					*Amount of Aid Awarded*					
	Women		*Men*		*All Athletes*	*Women*		*Men*		*All Athletes*	
Institution Type	*Number*	*%*	*Number*	*%*	*Number*	*Dollars*	*%*	*Dollars*	*%*	*Dollars*	*%*
Rural											
Small	898	37	1,521	63	2,419	1,557,472	7	2.202.420	8	3,759,890	8
Medium	4,119	9	6,499	61	10,618	7,635,129	36	10,820,096	41	18,455,225	39
Large	2,251	4	2,925	57	4,913	5,772,811	27	6,998,733	27	12,771,545	27
All rural	7,268	40	10,945	60	18,213	14,965,412	71	20,021,249	76	34,986,66	74
Suburban											
Single campus	868	50	885	50	1,753	1,304,438	6	1,228,233	5	2,532,671	5
Multicampus	891	46	1,045	54	1,936	2,195,117	10	2,551,180	10	4,746,298	10
All Suburban	1,759	48	1,930	52	3,689	3,499,555	17	3,779.413	14	7,278,969	15
Urban											
Single campus	378	43	511	57	889	648,889	3	733,316	3	1,382,207	3
Multicampus	933	45	1,139	55	2,072	1,951,510	9	1,843,243	7	3,794,752	8
All Urban	1,311	44	1,650	56	2,961	2,600,399	12	2,576,561	10	5,176,959	11
Grand Total	10,338	42	14,525	58	24,863	21,065,366	44	26,377,223	56	47,442,588	100

Note: Percentages may not add up to 100 percent due to rounding.

Table 9.3. Average Number of Students Receiving Athletic-Related Aid, Average Total Dollars Spent on Aid, and Average Award per Athlete, by 2005 Carnegie Basic Classification, 2003–2004

	Average Number Receiving Athletic-Related Aid			*Average Total Amount Spent on Athletic-Related Aid*			*Average Award per Athlete*	
Institution Type	*Women*	*Men*	*Total*	*Women*	*Men*	*Total*	*Women*	*Men*
Rural								
Small	26	45	1	$47,196	$64,777	$110,585	$1,734	$1,448
Medium	32	50	82	59,649	84,532	143,064	1,854	1,665
Large	35	46	81	91,632	109,355	199,555	2,565	2,393
All rural							2,059	1,829
Suburban								
Single campus	29	30	58	43,481	40,941	84,422	1,503	1,388
Multicampus	36	42	77	87,805	102,047	189,852	2,464	2,441
All suburban							1,990	1,958
Urban								
Single campus	25	34	59	43,259	48,888	92,147	1,717	1,435
Multicampus	27	33	59	57,397	52,664	108,421	2,092	1,618
All urban							1,984	1,562
Grand total	31	44	75	64,224	79,689	142,899	2,038	1,816

Note: Percentages may not add up to 100 percent due to rounding.

Coaching, Recruitment, and Overall Expenses

The Office of Civil Rights within the U.S. Department of Education identified eleven program areas, in addition to student interest and ability and student athletic aid, as areas that could be reviewed for compliance with Title IX. Of those areas, this study lends insight into recruitment and coaching specifically. However, due to space limitations and concerns over the quality of data on individual college athletic revenues and expenses, only limited results are reported here.

Examination of coaching reveals lingering inequity in community college athletics. Individuals who coach women's teams are compensated at a lower level than those who coach men's teams. The number of full- and part-time coaches employed by community colleges had low levels of variability. Most teams had a head coach who worked at least half-time. For men, the teams with the highest average number of full-time coaches were football and cross country, with an average of one full-time coach. For women, only track (indoor, outdoor, and cross country combined) rated one full-time coach. Women's golf had the lowest average for full-time coaches at 0.3 full-time equivalents (FTE); lacrosse was a close second at 0.4 head coach FTE. By comparison, swimming and ice hockey each averaged 0.6 FTE and had the lowest head coach averages among men's teams (Castañeda, 2004). At the assistant coach level, greater parity among men's and women's teams was demonstrated. Basketball, bowling, outdoor track and field, water polo, and softball and baseball had an equal average for men and women. Six of the fifteen sports played by both men and women had equal average staffing at the position of assistant coach. Golf, rodeo, and all track combined each had 0.2 assistant coach FTE or less for both the men's and women's teams. In contrast, football had 4.8 assistant coach FTE (Castañeda, 2004).

Relatively few financial dollars are spent in recruitment per sport, but inequity is still present in the allocation of those funds in an absolute sense. Nationally public community colleges spent more money recruiting male athletes, $1.6 million, than female athletes, $1.2 million. The average amount spent on new athlete recruitment per college was $2,955 and $2,197 for all men's teams and women's teams, respectively. Recruitment expenses for men and women indicate that although the colleges spend a higher gross amount on getting male athletes to campus, they spend a higher amount per female athlete. This is likely indicative of the public community college's efforts to comply with Title IX. Since female student athletes are more likely than their male counterparts to meet overall NCAA core course, grade point average, and test requirements (National Center for Fair and Open Testing, 2004), opportunities for athletic scholarships at four-year colleges may be greater for female than male athletes. According to Thein (2004), the result of NCAA Proposition 16 is that one-fourth of college seniors are no longer eligible to compete in NCAA varsity athletics.

Consequently community colleges must offer greater amounts of athletic-related student aid to female athletes than male athletes.

Average expenses for men's athletics teams were over 2.5 times that for women in 2003–2004. Some of this is likely due to the inequities caused by football, the most expensive of sports to sponsor, at an average just short of $100,000 per year. This compares to the most expensive sport for women, basketball, which averaged $38,703 per year. Both baseball and men's basketball had higher expenses than the most costly women's sport, basketball.

Recommendations for Policy and Practice

With over seventy-two thousand students participating, it is likely that intercollegiate athletics may be the most popular student activity in U.S. community colleges. Accordingly, community colleges will need to be responsive and offer expanded student activities, including athletics. Continued attention to compliance with Title IX is therefore essential for community colleges, given the potential severity of losing the ability to award financial aid as a consequence of violations (Mumford, 2006).

The decision of whether to offer scholarships for athletes is a weighty one that can affect a college's success in recruiting all students, and athletes particularly. Offering athletic financial aid can be a significant portion of the college's budget. And staffing decisions, such as whether to hire full- or part-time coaches and what to pay them, are made by high-level administrators and can be scrutinized under the lens of Title IX. Community college leaders must be vigilant about gender equity, especially in the light of the growing imbalance in college student enrollment, with women accounting for approximately 60 percent of all students.

The U.S. Department of Education has provided several options for how colleges can demonstrate compliance with gender equity as required in Title IX. This latest guidance allows colleges to assess student interest through an electronic survey and allows for nonresponses to be interpreted as a lack of interest (U.S. Department of Education, 2005). However, the NCAA (2005) promptly urged the Education Department to rescind the memo, fearing potential loss of hard-fought gains in women's athletics. We therefore offer the following options for colleges:

- Colleges should add sports, carefully choosing to maximize impact per dollar spent. Adding sports that share facilities, such as volleyball, basketball, or soccer, can help control expenses. Partnerships with local community centers for facilities use can reduce costs. Low-cost sports such as bowling can use outside facilities. If the college already has a track, adding track and field can be economical, averaging just $2,300 in expenses per women's team. Bowling is economical, but finding competition outside the Northeast can be difficult.

- Colleges should work within local leagues or athletic associations to add the same sports to area colleges all at once, to reduce travel expenses while increasing competition.
- Community colleges should increase opportunities for athletes. The NJCAA reported an increase of over thirty-three hundred female athletes in the ten years between 1990 and 2000. During this same time period there was a decline of over twenty-three hundred male participants in NJCAA competitions (NJCAA, 2002).
- Community college leaders should be both mindful and fair when it comes to establishing coaches' salaries and assistant coach staffing levels. Inequities in staffing levels and salaries between men's and women's sports can result in noncompliance with Title IX.
- The three existing community college athletic associations—the NJCAA, the Northwest Association, and the California Community Colleges—would benefit from working together to lobby Congress and the U.S. Department of Education's Office of Civil Rights for gender-equity tests that take into account the differences in enrollment patterns and student demographics between four-year and two-year colleges.

It is clear that intercollegiate athletics at community colleges are popular, yet the challenge of gender equity remains. Community colleges show commitment to achieving gender equity in their funding of athletic-related aid, the number of teams sponsored, the proportion of funds allocated to women's athletics, and the average recruitment expenditures for women athletes. Challenges still remain regarding the proportionality of participation, coaching levels and salaries, and overall expenditures. In conclusion, we agree with Duderstadt, who in 2000 wrote, "Gender equity is clearly the right goal for higher education. It is not only possible, but imperative if athletics are to play a legitimate role on our campuses."

References

American Association of University Professors. *The Faculty Role in the Reform of Intercollegiate Athletics: Principles and Recommended Practices.* Washington, D.C.: American Association of University Professors, 2002.

Ashburn, E. "To Increase Enrollment, Community Colleges Add More Sports." *Chronicle of Higher Education,* July 6, 2007, p. A31.

Bennion, S. D. *Junior College Athletics: Participation Opportunities and Academic Accountability.* In B. I. Mallette and R. D. Howard (eds.), *Monitoring and Assessing Intercollegiate Athletics.* New Directions for Institutional Research, no. 74. San Francisco: Jossey-Bass, 1992.

Berson, J. S. "Student Perceptions of the Intercollegiate Athletic Program at a Community College." Paper presented at the Annual Convention of the National Association of Student Personnel Administrators, Atlanta, Ga., Mar. 1996.

Campbell, R. C. "Rewarding Athletic Excellence Is Both Fair and Wise." *Ohio Association of Two-Year Colleges Journal,* 1988, *14*(1), 33–34.

Campion, W. J. "The National Junior College Athletic Association: A Study in Organizational Accountability." *Community College Review,* 1990, *17*(4), 47–51.

Carnegie Foundation for the Advancement of Teaching. *Basic Classification Descriptions, 2006*. Stanford, Calif.: Carnegie Foundation for the Advancement of Teaching, 2006.

Castañeda, C. "A National Overview of Intercollegiate Athletics in Public Community Colleges." Unpublished doctoral dissertation, University of North Texas, 2004.

Cohen, A. M., and Brawer, F. B. *The American Community College*. (4th ed.) San Francisco: Jossey-Bass, 2003.

Dempsey, C. W. *President to President: The Will to Act Project*. Indianapolis, Ind.: National Collegiate Athletic Association, 2002.

Duderstadt, J. J. *Intercollegiate Athletics and the American University*. Ann Arbor: University of Michigan Press, 2000.

Fields, R. R. *The Community College Movement*. New York: McGraw-Hill, 1962.

Fink, J. R., and Kirk, A. "Community College Athletics: The Road Less Traveled." *Educational Record*, 1979, *60*, 439–443.

Gavora, J. *Tilting the Playing Field: Schools, Sports, Sex and Title IX*. San Francisco: Encounter Books, 2002.

Gerdy, J. R. *The Successful College Athletic Program: The New Standard*. Phoenix, Ariz.: American Council on Education, 1997.

Koos, L. V. The *Junior College Movement*. Minneapolis: University of Minnesota Press, 1925.

Medsker, L. L. *The Junior College: Progress and Prospect*. New York: McGraw-Hill, 1960.

Monroe, C. R. *Profile of the Community College*. San Francisco: Jossey-Bass, 1972.

Mumford, V. E. "Promoting Equity and Access in Two-Year College Intercollegiate Athletic Programs." *Community College Journal of Research and Practice*, 2006, *30*(3), 213–222.

National Center for Fair and Open Testing. *Gender Bias in NCAA Eligibility Requirements*. Cambridge, Mass.: National Center for Fair and Open Testing, 2004.

National Collegiate Athletic Association. *In Honor of Title IX Anniversary, NCAA Urges Department of Education to Rescind Additional Clarification of Federal Law*. Indianapolis, Ind.: National Collegiate Athletic Association, 2005.

National Junior College Athletic Association (NJCAA). *NJCAA Handbook and Casebook 2002-2003*. Denver, Colo.: National Junior College Athletic Association, 2002.

Owiesny, C. L. "Gender Balance in Intercollegiate Athletics at California Community Colleges." Unpublished doctoral dissertation, San Jose State University, 2000.

Pollock, A., and Pingley, N. "An Alternative Athletic Program." *Community College Review*, 1986, *14*(3), 51–52.

RMC Research Corporation. *Title IX Athletics Compliance at California's Public High Schools, Community Colleges, and Universities*. Sacramento: California Postsecondary Education Commission, 2004.

Smith, D. "Athletic Programs in Ohio Two-Year Institutions: A Neglected Tool for Student Recruitment. *Ohio Association of Two-Year Colleges Journal*, 1987, *13*(2), 19–23.

Steiner, P. E., and Milander, H. M. "Changing the Emphasis upon Community College Athletics." *Community College Review*, 1978, *6*(1), 30–35.

Stokes, R. "The Presidential Role in Community and Junior College Athletics." *Educational Record*, 1979, *60*, 421–438.

Telander, R. *The Hundred Yard Lie: The Corruption of College Football and What We Can Do to Stop It*. Chicago: University of Illinois Press, 1996.

Thein, P. J. "Feather River College Original Feasibility Study for Additional Sports Programs with Follow-Up Data." Paper presented at the meeting of the American Association of Community Colleges, Minneapolis, Minn., Apr. 2004.

Thelin, J. R. *Games Colleges Play*. Baltimore, Md.: Johns Hopkins University Press, 1994.

Thornton, J. W. *The Community Junior College*. (3rd ed.) Hoboken, N.J.: Wiley, 1972.

U.S. Department of Education. *Digest of Education Statistics*. Washington, D.C.: U.S. Department of Education, 2002.

U.S. Department of Education. *Equity in Athletic Disclosure Act Survey 2003–2004*. Washington, D.C.: U.S. Department of Education, 2003.

U.S. Department of Education. *The Athletic Disclosure Website.* Washington, D.C.: U.S. Department of Education, 2004. Accessed Apr. 1, 2008, at www.ed.gov/finaid/prof/resources/athletics/eada.html.

U.S. Department of Education. *Additional Clarification of Intercollegiate Athletics Policy: Three-Part Test.* Washington, D.C.: U.S. Department of Education, 2005.

U.S. General Accounting Office. *Intercollegiate Athletics: Recent Trends in Teams and Participants in National Collegiate Athletic Association Sports.* Washington, D.C.: U.S. General Accounting Office, 2007.

CINDY CASTAÑEDA *is dean of ethnic studies, social science, and physical education at Richland College.*

STEPHEN G. KATSINAS *is professor of higher education administration and director of the Education Policy Center at the University of Alabama.*

DAVID E. HARDY *is assistant professor of higher education administration and director of research in the Education Policy Center at the University of Alabama.*

10

This final chapter reviews strategies that community colleges can use to address issues of gender and create more equitable and pluralistic environments. It also discusses the need for research that examines the intersection between social identities and community college mission, culture, and environment.

Strategizing for the Future

Pamela L. Eddy, Jaime Lester

The chapters in this volume review a variety of issues regarding gender at community colleges. The context of higher education provides the backdrop for how community college leaders and campus members see the issues they face and how they begin to make meaning of their location and experiences on campus. There is a wide variety of circumstances within community colleges that make the needs of each campus different. As campus members begin to think of strategies for the future, it is important for them to understand and identify the critical issues. This chapter summarizes critical areas facing two-year colleges, provides recommendations for future research, and reviews strategies for implementation.

Pressing Issues

Several areas of concern are pressing on American campuses. At the forefront of gender conversations have been assaults against affirmative action practices. In particular, Title IX restrictions and limitations have been enacted, and some states have passed legislation banning the use of affirmative action in hiring and admission decisions. At the same time, how we think about gender has expanded. No longer are gender issues strictly about women. The notion of the social construction of gender begins to blur the lines between the sexes. Baca Zinn, Hondagneu-Sotelo, and Messner (2005) conceptualized a matrix of the construction of gender, identifying over nine hundred permutations that can represent gender.

New Directions for Community Colleges, no. 142, Summer 2008 © 2008 Wiley Periodicals, Inc.
Published online in Wiley InterScience (www.interscience.wiley.com) • DOI: 10.1002/cc.329

Affirmative Action. Until the passage of Title IX of the Education Amendments of 1972 and other legislation passed that year, women and students were exempted or not covered by antidiscrimination laws. Title IX has long stood for the commitment to obtaining gender equity in education since it prohibited exclusion from participation in educational programs based on sex. In 2005, the Department of Education issued a Title IX clarification that allows schools to show compliance with the law using less rigorous measures that document compliance (U.S. Department of Education, 2005). The long-term effects of this change in policy remain unknown, but the loss of support for equality for women and girls raises concern.

Affirmative action is also under attack. The impetus for affirmative action was to redress long-standing discrimination against women and people of color in employment, education, and contracting decisions. In 1996, passage of Proposal 209 in California, which amended the state constitution, prohibited public institutions from granting preferential treatment based on race, sex, color, ethnicity, or national origin. More recently, the Michigan Civil Rights Initiative, or Proposal 2, passed, eliminating preferential treatment for previously protected groups, including women and individuals of color. Leading up to the passage of Proposal 2 in Michigan were two Supreme Court rulings regarding the admissions process at the University of Michigan. In the case of *Grutter* v. *Bollinger* (2003), use of affirmative action in admissions to the law school was upheld. However, the case of *Gratz* v. *Bollinger* (2003) determined that the undergraduate affirmative action admissions policy at the University of Michigan was too mechanistic and therefore unconstitutional.

Affirmative action opened the doors of college for many women and students of color. Title IX contributed to a marked increase in the participation of women in college and in college athletic programs in particular. Sadly, it has not been applied vigorously to many other areas of disparity, such as the low proportion of women faculty in areas like chemistry compared to the number of qualified women with doctorates in chemistry. The elimination of preferential treatment in hiring in California and Michigan may limit the ability of colleges and universities to recruit a more diverse student body or workforce.

Indeed, community colleges already have wide representation of women as students and faculty. Almost 60 percent of the study body is composed of women, and faculty are near parity, with 48 percent women and 52 percent men (National Center for Education Statistics, 2005). The community college has been a welcoming site for women returning to education after periods of absence and for students of color given its lower cost and increased access. Community colleges have also shown movement toward compliance with Title IX. In Chapter Nine, Castañeda, Katsinas, and Hardy found that females received near equal amounts of athletic aid despite the fact that they represented a little over one-third of the total number of athletes. Furthermore, there were almost equal numbers of intercollegiate athletic teams for women and men. Gains are still needed in salary equity for coaches and the number of female athletes, but community colleges are attempting to achieve equity and comply with Title IX.

Expansion of Gender Construction. Gender issues on campus are not limited to women. Recently attention has focused on the reversal of participation in postsecondary education by men. As noted, men are now in the minority of participants at community colleges, representing 40 percent of all students. Furthermore, African American men represent only 13 percent of the student body (National Center for Education Statistics, 2005). Instead, men more often seek employment directly out of high school. Although many indicators show both male progress and lack of progress in higher education, long-term evidence of male enrollment in college demonstrates that young males in high school are faring better than females and that men are enrolling and completing college in larger absolute numbers than previously. The overall picture cannot be reduced to the simplistic views of winners and losers that dominate much of the discussion of males in higher education today.

Another critical illustration of the gender gap concerns the participation of black and Hispanic students in postsecondary education. The gender gap has been shown to disfavor black and Hispanic students who were underrepresented in postsecondary education. Yet the declines in male enrollment are even across all race and ethnic categories, demonstrating a decrease in male enrollment despite race or ethnicity. In Chapter Two, Perrakis found that male students are more alike than different. Across racial groups, student outcomes and predictors of student success remained constant. Financial aid among black and Hispanic students also illustrates a conflicting pattern. Townsend (Chapter One) explains that 76 percent of blacks receive financial aid, but the majority of the aid is in the form of student loans. High levels of aid are important to promote persistence in college, but loan debt creates a significant burden for students once they complete college.

Harris and Harper (Chapter Three) also provide evidence of the unique experience of men in community college in a discussion of masculinity. The vignettes of male students in the chapter illustrate how gender socialization, which is connected to masculine notions of physical prowess, responsibility of providing financially for a family, and participation in sports, bears on academic success. Without support that validates the gender conflicts, male students often face academic and social difficulties in community colleges.

Recommendations for Future Research

The research reported in this volume points to several key findings. Townsend discussed the advances in thinking about gender in community colleges over the past decade. Key in her discussion is the fact that community colleges offer more parity in numbers for women in faculty ranks. Duggan (Chapter Five) found that the majority of staff members responding to her survey were women. Female respondents indicated they were more likely to have interactions with faculty and students and that they were satisfied with their jobs. When asked about work-life balance, Sallee (Chapter Eight) determined that those working at the case site chose a community college to obtain increased work-life balance. Issues facing campus members included child care and elder care responsibilities, with participants noting in particular the lack of policies to promote work-life balance. Eddy and Cox (Chapter Seven) concluded that despite larger numbers of women obtaining community college presidencies, parity was still not achieved. Furthermore, the gendered organization framework of community colleges reifies and values male norms, creating a disadvantage and deficit for women. Disparity was evident in athletics as well. Although Castañeda, Katsinas, and Hardy found that sports were equally available for both women and men at community colleges, participation numbers were not equal.

The research findings set out in this volume point to areas for future research. First, it is important to study the best practices that support an expanded notion of gender on campuses. The perception of more gender equity in the two-year college sector aids in creating a reality that these campuses are gender friendly. Although some of the research presented in this volume questions the extensiveness of this gender equity, it is clear that women are able to find advancement opportunities and job satisfaction at community colleges. Determining what best practices are most supportive and discovering how to replicate these programs on other campuses is needed.

Given the expanded definition of gender, it is important to conduct research on the points of intersection of race, class, and gender. The conception of community colleges as "democracy colleges" (Cohen and Brawer, 2003) lays a foundation of expectation that these institutions are receptive and open. Clearly community colleges provide opportunities for second chances for their students and enroll the highest percentages of minority students. Understanding more of the influence of the climate of the community college on future career paths for students and employees can enable leaders to be more purposeful in creating programs to promote women and individuals of color into administrative, staff, and faculty positions.

The career pathways for women in community colleges are serendipitous. Fugate and Amey (2000) found that faculty often happened upon their two-year colleges as career options versus purposefully seeking these career options. The presidents in Eddy and Cox's study did not start their careers with an intention of seeking a presidency. Their career sequencing to accommodate work-life balance was not always planned. More research is needed on the career pathways of staff, faculty, and leaders to understand the patterns inherent in careers based within two-year institutions. Furthermore, a fuller comprehension of policies and practices that promote women and individuals of color can be replicated on campuses. Moreover, appreciation of the barriers preventing advancement is important to allow more choices along the pipeline.

Collaborations among community colleges and regional four-year institutions can both share and pool best practices to support campus members.

The American Council on Education Office of Women in Higher Education provides national and regional forums to help prepare women for advanced leadership positions, with training open to women from both community colleges and four-year colleges.

Research is needed to determine key points in development practices for staff, faculty, leaders, and students. Development activities may reach a wide audience for participation and be relevant across job and status locations. Given the fact that many of the students at community colleges are adults, they are facing many of the same issues of child and elder care and work-life balance needs as are campus members. Understanding more of the impact of these policies on the populations will help.

Strategies for Practice

A number of programs can be implemented to target different populations within the community college. Following are suggestions for students, faculty, and leaders. Finally, overall policy suggestions provide a way of addressing potential organizational issues.

Students. One of the methods to address gender issues among students is to acknowledge the diversity of the student population and promote greater gender awareness and sensitivity. As open access institutions, community colleges enroll large numbers of students of color as well as students from various socioeconomic groups. One important suggestion to assist students who face identity conflicts is to provide a forum to discuss identity issues with a focus on the negative perceptions of help seeking that are often connected to gender socialization. Using journaling, media messages, and Internet blogs as examples of socialization may help to begin the discussion and spark dialogue. Campuses may also want to consider increasing the participation of students in campus programs to assist students in identifying with their role as college students and with the campus. Importantly, campuses need to collect data through interviews, focus groups, and surveys to assess student identity-specific needs.

The pervasive discussions of the gender gap among students and the low representation of women in science, technology, engineering, and math (STEM) fields illustrate that gender gaps still exist. Women are not entering the STEM fields, and the enrollment of males overall has decreased. Community colleges should create mentoring programs within high schools as well as between the college and community organizations. Several community colleges across the country have partnered with local organizations that seek to establish more women in vocational fields, such as welding and construction management. The community colleges match professional women with current students who job-shadow and interview women in the field. Students report feeling less isolated and more supported, and they have a more realistic idea of the field of their interest. Community college may also consider promoting TRIO programs (or other similar programs) within local high schools to target males. Community college can hold informational sessions, identify and recruit male students in need of additional aid to go to college, adopt a student group, or inform parents of the educational and economic gains male children will experience by attending college. Each of these programmatic efforts may promote the enrollment of males in postsecondary education and decrease the gender gap.

Faculty. The community college has historically shown parity between men and women in the faculty ranks, and Townsend notes that community colleges are more likely to be gender-equitable institutions compared to their four-year counterparts with respect to numbers of men and women in faculty positions. Despite the relative equity of community colleges, gender inequities remain, as evidenced by salary disparities, the low numbers of women in certain fields, and the lack of involvement of women on high-powered governance committees. Lester and Lukas (Chapter Six) demonstrated that women faculty show similar involvement in campus governance overall but are underrepresented on the governance committees that make budgetary, tenure, and promotion decisions. To address the disparities of faculty representation on key committees, community colleges need to conduct internal self-examinations, create benchmarks that promote the representation of women across all areas of the college, and empower faculty to advocate for change. Surveys and focus groups of faculty can assist in understanding which aspect of the climate prevents equal representation. From the self-study, policies that require the representation of men and women on governance boards or new practices in the faculty hiring process may emerge. Colleges should require that high-power committees have equal representation of men and women, as well as faculty of color. In addition, colleges need to empower faculty to become more involved and to advocate on behalf of the hiring of women and faculty of color. Creating training programs with a focus on faculty leadership and workshops on creating change can bring together like-minded faculty and promote the presence of change agents across the campus.

Another pressing concern among faculty that requires practical solutions concerns the number of part-time faculty. As Sallee noted, part-time faculty comprise more than half (63 percent) of the total number of faculty at community colleges, and many of those part-time faculty are women (49 percent). The large number of part-time faculty also has an impact on campus governance, which is reliant on the volunteer work of a small number of full-time faculty. The exclusion of part-time faculty is impractical, as part-time faculty are needed to maintain democratic colleges. Discussions need to occur to deconstruct biases that current full-time faculty and administrators hold that have prevented the inclusion of part-time faculty (Kezar, Lester, and Anderson, 2006). Many individuals believe that part-time faculty are not considered real faculty or that part-time faculty do not have an interest in the health of the college. Deconstructing these biases can get at the root of the systematic exclusion of part-time faculty and promote discussions of policy development and revision. Creating new or revising old policies will be met with resistance without time for deconstruction.

Leaders. One means to address gender equity within the leadership ranks is by leadership development training and intentional succession planning. Preceding the need for development is the requirement to redefine traditional leadership ideals. As Eddy and Cox pointed out, current expectations of the disembodied worker based on male norms (Acker, 1990) create a standard that marginalizes women. The community college literature is replete with examples of white men leading the institutions over time (Amey and Twombly, 1992), leaving little room for alternative role models. The situation for leaders of color is even starker. While community colleges boast the highest percentage of presidents of color at 14 percent, this number has changed little over the past decade and is not near the parity of numbers of students of color within two-year colleges. Community colleges also are held in regard for the number of women of color in the presidential office. Almost half (48 percent) of all women presidents of color are found at the community college (National Center for Education Statistics, 2005). In context, this percentage appears paltry since only 4.3 percent of all college presidents are women of color (Harvey and Anderson, 2005).

Leadership development should be a focus for succession planning on campus. The projected turnover in upper-level administrative ranks underscores a need to plan ahead. Over 45 percent of current community college presidents are sixty-one years of age or older (American Council on Education, 2007). The American Association for Women in Community Colleges provides an annual program that focuses on developing women in leadership positions, but not all women or campuses can support attendance to this conference. The limitations of current development opportunities underscore the need for community colleges to develop leadership training unique to them. This format allows cultural-specific development and more clearly aligns with institutional needs. The creation of campus or regional leadership academies can address needs. Particular attention can then be given to the construction of alternative models of leadership and the preparation for the leaders of the future (Kezar, Carducci, and Contreras-McGavin, 2006). Ethical leaders with cultural competencies and adaptive leadership abilities are required to lead the complex organizations of today. One model of leadership is no longer acceptable to meet current demands.

Policy. Individual campuses can develop policies to help support acceptance of a wider conception of gender roles. Policy can begin to remove structural barriers—for faculty, administrators, and students. Establishing guidelines for family leave policies eliminates the need for individual negotiation of time off (Wolf-Wendell, Ward, and Twombly, 2007). Family-friendly policies can begin to address concerns over work-life balance for campus employees. This model can then influence the appreciation for the balance that community college students negotiate every day with their multifaceted lives. Cluster hiring can expand opportunities for individuals of color and provide support for their work on campus. The creation of women's studies departments and centers and child care centers can symbolize the support of gender issues on campus.

The reality of fiscal demands puts pressures on institutions to support the full array of programs and projects to support gender issues on campus. Entering into regional compacts with other educational institutions can aid in meeting the demands of the college at a lower cost. The historic mission of community colleges to meet community needs is also fulfilled in these forms of partnerships. Community colleges should also support state and federal policies that foster the full participation of women and individuals of color.

Conclusion

This volume provides an update to gender research conducted since the publication of Townsend's 1995 volume of *New Directions in Community Colleges* that focused on gender. The research reported here shows that how we think of gender has expanded over time. Current pressures on gender advancement include restrictions on affirmative action and limitations on Title IX. Gender equity has not uniformly been obtained and certainly is uneven along the lines of race and ethnicity. A focus on intentionality needs to occur for gender advancements to continue. There remains a need for more gender-neutral organizations. Despite the increasing number of women in all avenues of the community college sector, male norms still dominate and serve as the measure for evaluation. This type of deficit model will mean that women will not be ideal workers since they still bear the major responsibilities for family care.

Individually, women can prepare and work toward change. Preparation can include getting the appropriate credentials required for advancement, advocating for family friendly work policies, and mentoring others to continue the progress made to date. Positional leaders can model a work ethic not based on the disembodied worker ideal (Acker, 1990), but one based on balance and that allows for expanded ways of learning. Those in upper-level positions can advocate for policy changes that make the workplace more gender friendly.

A need exists to educate hiring committees on merits of hiring someone not necessarily in the mold of the past. Glazer-Raymo (1999) highlighted how hiring boards tend to hire those who look like them, namely, white men. Moving beyond this practice can bring increased diversity to the community college sector.

We can be encouraged that we see marked changes in the thirteen years since Townsend's volume. However, the slow growth in women ascending to the community college president's office raises concerns over advancing equity. The effect of the erosion of affirmative action policies is not yet known. Thus, we need to be vigilant in working for equity for all.

References

Acker, J. "Hierarchies, Jobs, Bodies: A Theory of Gendered Organizations." *Gender and Society,* 1990, *4*(2), 139–158.

American Council on Education. *The American College President.* Washington, D.C.: American Council on Education, 2007.

American Council on Education, Office of Women in Higher Education. *Leadership Development Forums.* Washington, D.C.: American Council on Education, 2007.

Amey, M. J., and Twombly, S. B. "Revisioning Leadership in Community Colleges." *Review of Higher Education,* 1992, *15*(2), 125–150.

Baca Zinn, M., Hondagneu-Sotelo, P., and Messner, M. A. (eds.). *Gender Through the Prism of Difference.* (3rd ed.) New York: Oxford University Press, 2005.

Cohen, A., and Brawer, F. *The American Community College.* (4th ed.) San Francisco: Jossey-Bass, 2003.

Fugate, A. L., and Amey, M. J. "Career Stages of Community College Faculty: A Qualitative Analysis of Their Career Paths, Roles, and Development." *Community College Review,* 2000, *28*(1), 1–22.

Glazer-Raymo, J. *Shattering the Myths: Women in Academe.* Baltimore, Md.: Johns Hopkins University Press, 1999.

Gratz v. Bollinger, 539 U.S. 244 (2003).

Grutter v. Bollinger, 539 U.S. 306, (2003).

Harvey, W. B., and Anderson, E. L. *Minorities in Higher Education 2003–2004: Twenty-First Annual Status Report.* Washington, D.C.: American Council on Education, 2005.

Kezar, A., Lester, J., and Anderson, G. "Lacking Courage, Corporate Sellout, Not a Real Faculty Member: Challenging Stereotypes That Prevent Effective Governance." *NEA: Thought and Action,* 2006, *221,* 121–134.

Kezar, A. J., Carducci, R., and Contreras-McGavin, M. *Rethinking the "L" Word in Higher Education: The Revolution of Research on Leadership.* San Francisco: Jossey-Bass, 2006.

National Center for Education Statistics. *Digest of Education Statistics, 2005.* Washington, D.C.: U.S. Department of Education, 2005.

Townsend, B. K. (ed.). *Gender and Power in the Community College.* New Directions for Community Colleges, no. 89. San Francisco: Jossey-Bass, 1995.

U.S. Department of Education. *Additional Clarification of Intercollegiate Athletics Policy: Three-Part Test.* Washington, D.C.: U.S. Department of Education, 2005.

Wolf-Wendell, L., Ward, K., and Twombly, S. B. "Faculty Life at Community Colleges: The Perspective of Women with Children." *Community College Review,* 2007, *34*(4), 255–281.

PAMELA L. EDDY is associate professor in the department of educational leadership at Central Michigan University.

JAIME LESTER is assistant professor of higher education at George Mason University.

INDEX

YOUR free ISSUE OF NATIONAL CIVIC REVIEW

is now available online. Go to www.interscience.wiley.com/journal/NCR

WILEY InterScience®
DISCOVER SOMETHING GREAT

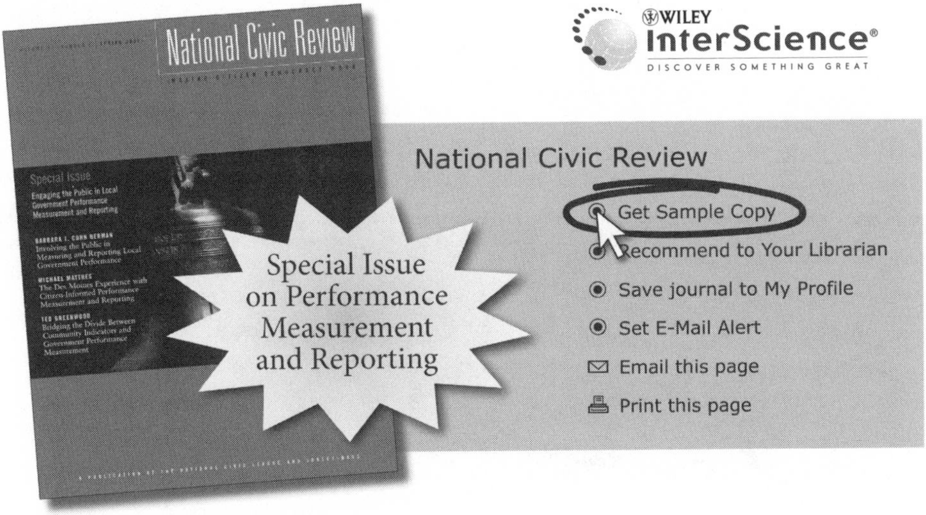

In this Issue:

- Public Employees as Partners in Performance: Lessons From the Field *by Brooke A. Myhre*
- Starting Performance Measurement From Outside Government in Worcester *by Roberta Schaefer*
- Current Approaches to Citizen Involvement in Performance Measurement and Questions They Raise *by Anne Spray Kinney*
- Bridging the Divide Between Community Indicators and Government Performance Measurement *by Ted Greenwood*

WILEY
Publishers Since 1807